FIRE: FINANCIAL INDEPENDENCE RETIRE EARLY

THE ULTIMATE GUIDE TO ACHIEVING FINANCIAL INDEPENDENCE SO YOU CAN RETIRE EARLY

DAVID JACOBS

INTRODUCTION

Let me ask you a question: What if you could wake up tomorrow and take a look at your bank account and realize that you've achieved financial independence? Would you like that? It's safe to say that is a rhetorical question. Pretty much everyone reading this book would like some of that!

Achieving financial independence isn't hard, however most humans lack the discipline to do so. Also, financial independence means different things to different people, which is why it is important to define what that term means to you. There is no easy way to answer this. Some might say a million dollars will guarantee them financial freedom while others might say 10 million would do the trick. Still, some others will struggle to assign a monetary value to it and consider qualitative factors as the most important.

Given that this is a personal question, I suppose a wide variety of responses are to be expected. There's no denying one fact though: If you're reading this book, chances are that you're tired of working at your job that doesn't reward you for your knowledge, skillset, and hard work. And in some cases, some of you may be living paycheck to paycheck with barely any savings or assets to show for.

There's nothing more soul-sucking than working a job and feeling that you are not progressing toward your financial goals. This is true even if you happen to love what you do. The fact is that almost everyone works a regular job because it's the easiest way to make money. You show up, you do the work, and you receive a paycheck at the end of every month.

The other part of the equation is that we've been taught to value stability and security over a lot of other things since childhood. The very fact that most of us go into debt to fund our college education that may or may not provide a good future for us is proof of this. While some of us are strong enough to go the entrepreneurial route, this isn't a suitable path for everyone.

In fact, quitting your full-time job and trying to start your own business is one of the worst things you can do, at least for most people who don't have the entrepreneurial mindset. Sure, you read about success stories all the time, but this is just survivor bias in action. In other words, you only read about the successes, not the heaping amounts of failed experiences that accompany them. Entrepreneurship is tough and risky. It has also been presented as the only way to achieve financial independence.

The glorification of the entrepreneurial hustle and laptop lifestyle has led to a lot of people fantasizing about how cool it would be to be their own boss and own a startup that is doing meaningful work. I'm here to tell you that you can start a company that installs toilets in every home in India and still lose money. Meaningful work alone doesn't guarantee profits. It takes a combination of a good idea, excellent execution, deep pockets, some serious grit and relationship building, and a little luck to get things going in business.

The truth is that most people are lacking in one of those areas and as such, the entrepreneurial world isn't for them. Does this mean they're doomed to a life of financial dependence? In other words, is it possible for an ordinary person such as you to achieve levels of wealth that will guarantee a life of freedom? Not at all! In fact, as you continue to read this book, you'll learn all you need to know about being financially savvy so you too can find financial freedom, whatever that looks like for you!

The Opportunity

I don't know how you came across this book or what motivated you to start reading it, but what I do know is that the internet has something to do with it. Perhaps you purchased an e-book or read the reviews online or whatever. My point is that the internet has closed the chasm between the 'haves' and "have-nots." It provides an equal opportunity and a level playing field to anyone who is willing to bet on themselves, their skills and talents, and work hard to make something of themselves!

Never has it been easier for people to start their own businesses and earn passive income from them. In addition to this, the sheer amount of information available on the internet has made it possible for us to live or vacation in Taiwan and run a real estate business in Dallas.

That last statement isn't a pipe dream. It's a fact and it aptly describes how I run my businesses these days. You see, ten years ago I was in your shoes. I probably had a worse job than yourself, earning a terrible wage, and fantasizing about all kinds of business ideas. At one point, I was willing to take a shot at sinking money into a "once in a lifetime opportunity" investing into a multi-level marketing business without realizing it was actually a pyramid scheme!

I'm sure you've felt this kind of desperation. It wasn't

that I was stupid. I was just tired of making little money and having it go nowhere by sitting in the bank. Speaking of banks, it wasn't too long ago when my bank notified me that they would be slashing the interest rates on my savings accounts because apparently they were in trouble over some mortgages.

The U.S government gave them free money to bail themselves out but I'm yet to see a single penny of that cash! Fast forward to today, and I can honestly call myself a global businessman. I use the word 'global' because I can travel wherever I want, whenever I want. My businesses are location independent and leverage the power of the internet.

The way I've gotten there is by applying the principles I'll teach you in this book. These principles have not only helped me get this far but have also ensured that I'll never have to go back to my old life of wishing and hoping for some windfall to improve my lot in life.

What I Will Show You

What have you dreamed of achieving in your life? I'm not talking about some deep spiritual goal here. I can't help you out in that department, I'm afraid. I can, however, show you exactly how the road to financial independence is achieved. The first step is to define what that is and what it means to you.

Far too many people attempt their journey without

figuring this out and it only leads them down winding paths that make it harder to achieve their goals. This is not going to be a mistake that you will make. Along with this, I will also show you how you can make real money. I'm not talking about some pie in the sky investing plan, but the real facts about the stock market and investing that no CFA is going to tell you.

I'd like to point out that I don't have any financial qualifications. All I have is my experience and my track record of success. I'm not going to pitch you any particular stocks or companies. Instead, my aim is to teach you *how* to invest your money in the safest and risk-free manner possible.

You might be thinking that 'risk-free' sounds a bit boring. After all, don't you need to risk a lot to gain a lot? No, you don't. This is a lie that has been forced upon you. The wealthy never take risks they can't afford to take. Instead, they focus on playing situations where the reward is far higher when compared to the risk. Over time, by playing these odds, they strike it big.

You're going to learn many life-changing principles in this book. All I ask in return is one thing: an open mind. You probably have some experience with the things I'm going to talk about in this book. Even if you do or consider yourself an expert at them, or even if you disagree, it's okay, I encourage you to read on with an open mind.

If I can empower you to take action and begin your journey of independence, I'll consider my job done. There really is no time like the present. This is both a fact and financial reality.

After all, common sense dictates that the sooner you begin dedicating yourself to growing your money, the larger the pile of cash that awaits you at the end of the road. So let's get started now and let's begin by learning how you too can achieve financial independence!

ARE YOU PREPARED FOR RETIREMENT? THE TRUTH CAN BE SCARY!

This chapter is not meant to be read as a horror story but you might come away with that impression. The fact remains that the traditional model of retirement is broken in America thanks to an unpredictable stock market and assets not earning as much as they once did.The days of corporations looking after their employees are long gone. Nowadays, you're even more of a number and an expense and most corporations look for ways to cut down costs, hence the layoffs and job losses. No matter how relationship-oriented a corporation can be, no matter how friendly and familial the work culture is, it's the numbers that really drive home the point.

So let's take a look, shall we?

· · ·

THE BEST CASE Scenario

I'm not going to tweak any numbers here to prove my point. In fact, what I'm going to do is take the best possible number from every category and paint a picture of what things can look like, assuming everything goes perfectly well. For the purposes of our example, let's try to project the amount a 21-year-old can realistically expect upon retirement at the age of 65.

For starters, we'll need to make some assumptions. We're trying to cover a long period of time here and some of these will be a bit unrealistic, but they'll give us a better picture overall. I'm going to assume that inflation in America is negligible. Inflation refers to the economic phenomenon whereby the price of goods keeps increasing over time.

For example, the price of a loaf of bread is far greater today than what it was in the 1960s. Inflation by itself isn't a bad thing as long as the increase in salaries keeps pace with it. However, when the latter lags behind, purchasing power declines. Guess what's happening in America these days?

Either way, we're going to go with a zero percent inflation rate. Next, I'm going to assume this 21-year-old kid has zero student debt which is yet another unrealistic expectation but it boosts the amount of savings she can squirrel away.

I'm going to assume a pre-tax salary of $56,516 for our college grad since this is the median household salary in America currently. Mind you, our 21-year-old is single but I'm going to give her an entire household's salary. Next, I'm going to assume her average savings per year amounts to 8%. Again, this is the national average savings rate.

I'm going to assume that her employer offers a 401(k) plan but doesn't match contributions. Company contributions boost returns quite a bit but are difficult to project due to varying situations. Also, if she happens to change jobs, which happens quite a lot these days, the rate of contributions will change. As a rule of thumb, I'm going to assume that an amount equivalent to 4% of her income goes into her 401(k) on a yearly basis.

THIS GIVES us the following numbers:

- Salary = $56,516
- Yearly savings (total) @8% of gross income = $4,521.28
- 401(k) contribution @4% of gross income = $2,260.24

Her 401(k) is tax-free which is good news and let's assume she's smart and invests in stock market index funds. These provide returns at a historic average of 8%. There are some other savings boosting assumptions I'm making here. Our 21-year-old is not going to buy a house or take out a mortgage on a home to live in.

Mortgages require significant down payments and while you get an asset in return, you'll learn in a later chapter why you might as well flush your money down the toilet if you decide to live in the home without earning cash from it. Either way, the lack of a mortgage or any significant life expenses boosts our 21-year-old's savings considerably.

She's earning 8% on her 401(k) on a yearly basis and retires at the age of 65. This gives her a total of $943,650 in her 401(k) which she can use to live out the rest of her years along with an additional $101,728 in cash in her savings account. All in all, she's got a cool net worth of $1,045,378 in the bank.

This is her best-case scenario assuming she matches the average that is currently prevalent in America. Assuming she keeps her cash as is in the bank and reinvests her 401(k) amount into bonds and funds that give her 8% returns per year, she can earn $75,492 per year before tax. Furthermore, assuming normal tax rates, this gives her a monthly income of $4,780 per month after taxes. All in all, that's not too bad. She can live comfortably, if not in luxury.

. . .

THE REAL WORLD

A lot of the income return we see in this example is generated thanks to the power of compound interest. The power of compound interest is evident when you consider that our fictional character's 401(k) balance amounts to just $276,579 when she's 50 years old. In the 15 years, from age 50 to 65, her savings grow exponentially from this amount to the final figure of $943,650.

To make compound interest work for you, you'll need to leave your principle untouched for as long a time as possible. This is not quite possible in the real world. Let's say our 21 year old has student loans that result in her savings being reduced to zero until the age of 30, something which is a reality for most Americans.

This reduces her 401(k) nest egg to a final value of $420,709. 8% returns on this is a paltry $33,656 per month or $2,804 per month before taxes. This is the effect of student loans lasting for just ten years and eating away all savings. We haven't even begun to estimate the effects of medical emergencies or other events that require cash expense.

A mortgage is a significant expense in everyone's lifetime. Let's say our 21 year old and her partner are less than savvy and follow the American dream and finance a home for themselves to live in. Usually, Americans purchase a home around ages 26-30 and finance for 30 years.

For simplicity's sake, I'm going to assume our person in question does so at the age of 35 and foots half the downpayment on the home, with the other half being covered by her partner. By this point in time, she has $11,303 in cash savings and $14,323.25 in her 401(k). Let's say they like the look of a $200,000 home, which happens to be the median home value in the United States (United States Home Prices & Values, 2020).[1]

They need to pay 20% of this as a downpayment which equates to $50,000. This means our person in question is liable to pay $25,000. She has no option but to break her 401(k) and withdraw some of her savings, some-thing that a lot of people do. Let's take it easy on her and assume she won't be hit with tax penalties for this.

This leaves her with a 30 year mortgage that she will pay off only when she's 65 (assuming she doesn't refi-nance) and a 401(k) balance of $626.45. At the age of 65, she's going to own a home that's too big for her to live in and a final 401(k) balance of $282,883.

This equates to a yearly return of $22,630 (at 8%) or $1,885 per month before taxes. She could sell the house and live on that money but this assumes the real estate market will continue to trend upward and that there won't be a crash of some kind. Taxes on her 401(k) income will amount to 17% roughly.

This leaves our former 21-year-old, who has worked her way out of student loans that funded her college and also now owns a piece of the American dream (her very own home!), with a paltry $1,565 per month income when she turns 65. Some retirement, huh!

I haven't even assumed healthcare costs, the costs of tuition for her children, emergency medical care in the family, home maintenance expenses, and other miscellaneous items that add up over time. I've assumed average to above-average rates every step of the way and all she can make is $1,500 per month.

How would you like to slave away for your boss for 45 years and be told that you need to now live on less than $2,000 per month?

FOLLOWING *The Rules*

What were you told about money when you grew up? My guess is that you were given the spiel about working hard, getting good grades, getting a good job, settling down, and then saving a little money away every month. This, you were told, would ensure that you would achieve freedom at retirement and at that point, you'd be able to do whatever you want.

Meanwhile, you saw the rich kid next door barrel around in his Corvette that was gifted to him. The fact is that the standard narrative espoused to the middle class in America no longer applies. The rich have become richer while the middle class are now officially the lower middle class. In many ways, it's worse to be a part of the middle class than poor.

You see, the middle class is all about being average. The name itself denotes this. Additionally, the middle class often pays the most in taxes despite not being in the highest tax bracket. The middle class is the one that receives the least number of tax breaks. In modern America, the middle is at the bottom.

I don't mean to say that it's great to be poor. Just like with the middle class, the poor have had to deal with even worse conditions. However, the government does step in and provide aid programs for the people who qualify. The middle class suffers from being perceived as being well off, but actually isn't.

It isn't out of the ordinary to see your average middle class family living paycheck to paycheck thanks to following the rules they've been told to follow by the generations that came before them. Get this into your head: That version of America no longer exists. Our society is no longer an equal opportunity utopian paradise it once was (or as close to it as it got).

These days, corporations dictate policy and the rich get

to keep their millions. Meanwhile, you are stuck with the bill for social services and are then told you're ineligible to receive benefits once you retire. Thank you for your service.

Student Loans

One of the biggest contributors to this savings crisis in America is the amount of student debt currently present. In our example, we assumed our 21 year old would pay off her loan by the age of 30. Turns out, this is a rather optimistic view. There are college graduates who are realistically looking at a lifetime of debt.

And for what? A piece of paper that says they attended some school and studied something. Most college graduates of this generation have either seen themselves graduate right as the economy fell apart in a recession or as jobs vanished thanks to outsourcing and the tech revolution.

The economy and our lives and lifestyle have changed at a pace that is unprecedented. The world doesn't have the air of stability it did back in the 60s and 70s when even a factory worker was guaranteed a steady pension and healthy retirement. A college degree, unless it happens to be from a prestigious institution and in a field that really needs it, is no longer worth the paper it's printed on or the hefty price tag.

I don't mean to say that college is worthless but it has become more essential than ever to evaluate the reward versus the costs of a college education. Colleges have always been about making money and have never denied this, even if they don't directly admit it. Furthermore, the elite colleges of America, the so-called Ivy League colleges, have policies that make social mobility extremely difficult.

'Legacy' applicants (applicants whose family members are alumni of the college) receive priority upon application and form the overwhelming number of graduates. Unless you happen to be a mountain player who plays the electric guitar, you can pretty much forget about attending these schools.

This means the jobs you apply to will be of a lesser quality and will have less security. Thus, social mobility is greatly reduced and getting truly rich is not possible. Surely, it no longer makes sense to follow the rat race or give in to the status quo of "go to school, get a job, and everything will be fine!"

Personally, it sounds like something a con artist would say.

THE WAIT For Freedom

One of the more annoying

portions of the standard narrative is that a person needs to wait before they get to cash in their hard work and attain freedom. For some reason, everybody needs to wait till they're 65 years old, or at least 60, before they can even think of retiring and living the life they've always wanted.

It's almost blasphemous to suggest or ask why a 35 year old can't do the same. Truth be told, to those who follow these tired old rules and philosophies it is unfathomable to think of a 35-year-old who can achieve this. Inundated and primitive thinking or rigid paradigms produce the same exact results and cycle such as the one you saw in the previous example.

Some people even consider retiring to less developed countries in an attempt to reduce their cost of living. They're willing to trade in less developed infrastructure, fluid political situations (to put it mildly,) less mobility, worse healthcare all because of affordability concerns. You'll often find these people speak of how pure the underdeveloped world is (perhaps true to an extent) when the reality is that they can barely afford a plane ticket back home!

There are some people who live this way by choice, of course. However, I can guarantee you that such people did not get there by following the commonly accepted rules. The only guaranteed place you will end up in if you do so is the line at the social security office, waiting your turn to apply.

UNCERTAINTY

I've touched previously upon the fact that our society is changing at a pace that has never been seen thus far in human history. If you're in college right now, the chances that your job or skill set will be automated and performed by machines is very likely. It's gotten to the point where machines are building other machines and human intervention is hugely reduced.

This has changed the nature of the workplace as well. Consider the fact that Amazon treats its warehouse employees like they're machines with everything down to the number of steps they take being measured and analyzed, as if everything was a question of analytics.

Employers increasingly demand recruits who can work like machines and this makes the workplace an oppressive place to be. Is it any wonder that trust in companies and institutions is at an all time low and workplace satisfaction and employee morale matches that level?

The Way Forward

Admittedly, all of this paints a pretty bleak picture. Perhaps you might feel that achieving financial independence is impossible given that the entire system is stacked against you. To that I always say: Every problem brings with it an opportunity waiting to be explored.

While it's true that the digital revolution has changed the way workplaces operate, it has also opened up streams of revenue that were unimaginable even ten years ago. While stock markets are more unstable than ever, the corporate heavy focus of government means that stocks as a bunch are engineered to skyrocket more than ever. This doesn't mean they'll do so overnight. It's just that the long term prospects for business in America are better than they have ever been, despite other countries catching up.

The average college degree might be devalued but this means you don't need to study or continue learning to secure a job anymore, unless you really want to. For instance, just because your father had to choose between his passion of French art history versus the stone cold reality of an accounting degree, you don't need to make that choice. There are multiple streams of revenue open to you that neither of you can fathom.

What has really changed are the underlying rules. *This* is the basis upon which FIRE (Financial Independence

- Retire Early) operates. You cannot get massive results by following the old rules. What you need is a framework that is applicable to this day and age. It's time for you to let go of those tired old tropes and begin to think in a new way.

In other words, you need to ask yourself: What's really important to me?

---

1. United States Home Prices & Values. (2020). Retrieved 27 January 2020, from https://www.zillow.com/home-values/

2

WHAT IS YOUR 'WHY?'

*E*very journey begins for a reason and the steps you've decided to take toward attaining financial freedom are no different. You see, you can receive the best financial plan out there which will grow your wealth but unless you have the right mindset in place, you're not going to be able to make it work.

So what is the right approach to take and what is the right mindset for you to adopt? More importantly, where do you begin?

WHY YOU NEED A 'WHY'

Money is an emotional topic for a lot of us. After all, money is what ensures our basic needs are fulfilled. Without it, shelter, food, and many

other basic necessities become uncertain and survival becomes an issue. This is why we put up with terrible jobs and even worse, tyrannical bosses after all.

The curious thing about money is that once a person begins to earn a certain amount of it, their focus shifts dramatically away from it. In other words, once this threshold is breached, qualitative things take center stage in life. The only exception to this is when a person has deep seated insecurities about money and links it to their sense of self worth.

Thus when addressing the issue of financial independence, it's important to move beyond the money and ask yourself why do you really want it in the first place? Too many people focus on the "how much" aspect of it, but do not pay enough attention to the underlying reason of why this amount of money is so important.

What will you do with it? Will you buy a house, fund your child's education, buy your folks a better home, and so on? These are deep questions so before getting into this, let's try to see if we can figure out the "how much" side of things.

How Much Do You Need?

Research indicates that for most people, the threshold of financial satisfaction lies at an absurdly low $75,000 per year. Mind you, this is not the financial independence threshold but merely what it takes to feel secure financially and feel that there's money in the bank to be able to weather any major storms.

The question of how much you need to be independent requires you to take a look at the kind of lifestyle you want to lead. This is a fun exercise to carry out. Where do you want to live and what kind of facilities do you want in your life? Do you want to be a digital nomad, traveling around the world? Or do you want to live in a penthouse in Manhattan?

There's no wrong answer here so don't censor yourself. Some of your answers might seem ridiculous but remember that this is your life. Aim for what truly moves you and appeals to you, no matter how crazy or unattainable it sounds. Once you have this picture down, you can reverse-engineer exactly how much you need and the action steps needed to get you there.

The digital nomad lifestyle is something that a lot of people aspire to. The thought of traveling through Southeast Asia and relaxing on beaches all day sounds fun. Of course, the reality is far different but we're only in the imagination stage at this point so it's all good. Traveling around the world is actually nowhere near as expensive as it sounds and I'll show you exactly how I manage to do this in a few chapters' time.

For now, your first step is to assess the living expenses in the destination of your choice and get a feel for how much you need to spend. For example, a country like Thailand will require monthly expenses of $1,000 and above in order for you to live well. That same amount will allow you to live like a king in a country like Vietnam. In contrast, $1,000 will confine you to some student hostel hovel in a place like Berlin.

Add to this the cost of airfare and living expenses and you'll begin to get a ballpark of how much you need to spend per month. Now go ahead and double that figure and that's your ballpark estimate of the after-tax income you need to earn per month. Add your tax rate to that figure and there's your financial threshold amount!

Obviously, this number is not going to remain constant throughout your life. As your income grows, so will your aspirations. This is perfectly fine. It's just money after all. You can always make more of it and the world is full of opportunities for you to explore.

Now that your amount is sorted, let's take a look at your why.

The Why(s)

Ask yourself *why* you want financial independence is a far more critical thing. Your first response might be, "I want to stick it to my boss!" This is a noble emotion to possess but it's a short term thing. What are you going to do once you walk out the door of your workplace? Have you considered what you will do while you're working toward your goal?

You'll most likely have to keep your current job. My point is that a lot of people get seduced by the euphoria that short term goals provide. Things such as sticking it to the man, getting to call oneself an "entrepreneur" or " self-employed," living a dream lifestyle etc., get most people carried away to the point where they ignore long term realities.

Too many people quit their existing stable lives to pursue their dreams of independence. Few that do this make it. In fact, it is those who keep as many options on the table instead of taking drastic action that are the most successful. You should think in long term qualitative terms when it comes to your goals instead of focusing on the short term.

The first few days after you walk out of your job will be spent in a bliss of doing nothing. After those few days though, you're going to have an itch you can't scratch. There's only so much lolling around you can do before you go crazy. The 'why' of your financial independence plan goes back to your purpose in life. What is it that you really want?

A good exercise is to ask yourself what the 5 year old version of yourself was crazy about! Your passion will not always match up with your activities at that age but more often than not, there will be a tangible connection. The key is to explore your passions. Perhaps you've been meaning to take that cooking class for a while? Who knows, if you get good enough at it, a career as a private yacht chef awaits?

You never know where life will end up taking you so be open to whatever comes you way. I must mention that you need to do all this while maintaining stability. You cannot focus on your passion if you're unsure where your next paycheck is going to come from. Manage your time well and soon, you'll see multiple income streams open up to you.

Often, your passion could be an idea or a lifestyle instead of a particular thing. For example, you might want to experience the freedom of location independence and feel the emotion of having the entire world opening itself up to you, ready to be explored. In such cases, you need to understand that you'll need to develop skills that will get you paid as you do this. In other words, you can't be a factory worker and expect to travel the world and work at the same time.

Some people cannot think of anything beyond a particular event or destination in their lives. Perhaps you want to explore some country and can't think of anything else. Whatever it is, suspend your judgment and go with whatever moves you the most. This is what will fuel you in the long run.

Long term goals such as these are hard to hit and require a good degree of emotion behind them. More than logic, emotion is what fuels us the most, which is why you need to harness that force. This is the power of your 'why.'

THE MINDSET

Your mindset underlines everything that you do. After all, your actions are the result of your thoughts and beliefs. The problem with our beliefs is that they sit in our subconscious mind and we are usually unaware of how they influence us. Awareness of our beliefs is the first step to solving any blocks or issues that are holding us back.

The second step is to adopt a set of actions that will help you tide over these harmful beliefs. Action, and not overthinking each action, is what helps you move forward and creates new beliefs in your mind. Action is what invalidates old beliefs that hold you back. It isn't enough for you to simply recognize limiting beliefs; you need to install new ones in their place. Taking action does this for you.

Here are some guidelines that will help you figure out the right way to behave. These actions will put you on the path of success. While your external world will take some time to change and adjust, remember that it is what's within you that counts the most. Your external results will take some time to catch up to what's going on inside. So don't be discouraged if you find that your results lag behind where you think you truly are, often external changes reflect what goes on within us. This is just how it is.

Decide

All great journeys start with a decision. Take some time right now and write down what kind of life you want to have. Who will be in this life? Where will you live? By when do you see yourself achieving this lifestyle? Some people have issues with putting a timeline on goals. One reason for this is fear. It can be disappointing to set a goal with a specific timeline and see that deadline pass you by.

Despite this, giving your goals a timeline forces you to acknowledge their existence and prevents you from slacking off. Those who don't have any problem being self-motivated face a different issue when it comes to timelines. They treat the timeline itself as a goal and don't provide any space for the universe to work its magic.

You don't know how life is going to unfold. You might set out for goal A and find that goal B is what really makes sense for you. Don't stick to goal A in the name of being 'determined' or 'tough.' The world will give you many clues and will make way for your true talents to emerge once you begin your journey. Use the timeline as a way of pushing yourself towards a particular goal. Once it stops making sense, do not hesitate to drop it.

Create *a Massive Action Plan*

"Massive action" is a phrase that was popularized by the motivational speaker Tony Robbins. The premise is simple. If regular actions get you to your goal within, say two years, it stands to reason that higher levels of action will get you there in half the time or less. Therefore, if you want to reach your goals quickly, take massive amounts of action.

Aside from getting there faster, there are other benefits of taking messy, massive action. One of the most underrated aspects of it is the ability to figure out quickly what's working and what isn't. As I mentioned earlier, you might set out for goal A and find that goal

B is what truly motivates you. In such cases, it's in your best interests to figure this out as soon as possible.

In other words, if you can figure out that A is bad for you in a few days as opposed to a few years, you've saved a ton of time. Time is the only resource you'll never get back and it is in your interest to use it as wisely as possible. Massive action does this for you.

So what does taking massive action look like? Contrary to what you might be thinking, massive action levels are relative. Someone who is used to doing five things in a day would be taking massive action if they double those levels. Someone who is used to doing just one thing a day might reach massive action levels by tripling that output.

It's all relative and the way to figure this out is to decide to take massive action by reminding yourself of your 'why.' Once this is done, at the end of each day, ask yourself if you truly took massive action or not. If you feel a sense of disappointment, you're probably not pushing yourself as much as you know you can.

Change *Your View*

Consider this, two people have a glass of water placed in front of them with the water at the halfway mark and are asked to describe the level of water in the glass. One of them says it's half full and the other says it's half empty. Perspective plays a huge role in our lives and the one you choose to adopt is crucial for your results.

You can look at yourself and think that you don't have the track record or ability to make great investment decisions. Or you can tell yourself that you are an intelligent person who can take correct decisions once you learn the right way to do things (which is what you're doing right now). It's entirely up to you.

You can view situations as problems or challenges—one feels more empowering than the other, I'll leave it to you to guess which one that is. They're either things that slow you down and cause you stress or force you to grow. It's all down to your perspective. Err on the side of positivity at all times. I'm not asking you to ignore the negatives or to stop being realistic. Acknowledge any obstacles and shortcomings you might face. Just recognize that there is never a situation that is 100% negative.

Always take action toward mitigating the negatives in a situation while acknowledging that you can see the positives. Focus on the solution and not the problem, and never ever think of yourself as being the victim. Placing a "poor me" label on yourself is one of the most unhelpful things you can do because it robs you of your power and prevents you from recognizing the immense abilities you have within you.

Again, I'm not asking you to walk around with a smile

plastered on your face at all times or to ignore all logic, reality, and possible hurdles. The point is to bring balance back to your views and choose to focus on the positives and the solutions while acknowledging that negatives exist, as they always do.

GET *Close to Fear*

Here's the thing: You're going to be afraid most of the time. That's just how change works. Instead of fearing fear, you need to flip the script and become close to it, befriend it. View fear as an ally instead of an adversary. In most situations, the presence of fear indicates that you should probably be taking action.

The reason this mindset works is because fear never goes away. Even after you've achieved financial independence, it'll always be there because it is a part of being human. The next time you feel fear, take some time to examine how you feel physically. If you have the time, write down what was running through your mind and allow yourself to feel it completely. Don't run away from any emotion that surfaces, instead, honor it and allow it to pass.

Contrast it with how you felt some time later, once it dissipated. Did your worst fear realize itself? Were you exaggerating things? How do you feel right now depending on whether you took action or not? Taking note of your observations and writing them in a notebook or digital note app is a great way to check in with your mind and gain awareness of what you can do better.

CREATE ROUTINES

Habits are what help you stay dedicated to your dreams and goals. They keep you on the track to success. Ask yourself, what are your habits right now? Take the time to write down what you do starting from the moment you wake up till the moment you go to sleep. Do your habits and actions help you achieve the things you want in life?

Or are you practicing habits that cause you to drift around aimlessly? Frustration is a sign of you not living up to your potential. The key is to recognize this frustration for what it is (a symptom) and to use it as a motivator to create rituals and habits that push you to higher highs.

A great habit to engage in the morning, soon after you wake up, is to read out a bunch of positive statements to yourself. Alternatively, you can visualize your perfect lifestyle and get in touch with how that makes you feel. When you wake up, do you curse the new day or do you welcome it with open arms? Do you run through a list of all the stuff you need to do or do you take the time to remind yourself of everything that is great in your life?

Shift your life perspective and see how much better your day becomes. Along the way, you'll find yourself carrying out actions and habits that will push you to higher levels.

CHOOSE *Your Environment*

The people around you have a huge impact on the kind of results you will see in your life. Research indicates that the five people you interact with the most will have a profound impact on your life. However, it's not as simple as that. The five people that your "circle of five" interacts with will also influence you indirectly and so on until there's a whole web of strangers you're indirectly in touch with thanks to those around you.

There is nothing to be gained by willingly interacting with negative people or those who don't have your best interests at heart. Sometimes, they will have your best interests at heart but are themselves far too afraid to take action or inspire you positively. In such cases, it is best to minimize contact or put some physical distance between the two of you so that your contact with them is limited to certain times of the week.

The environment you live in also shapes how you think and behave. If you're someone who loves mountain air, but finds herself living in the swamps of Florida, it's safe to say you're going to be a little miserable. I'm not saying you should pack up and move immediately, but set an intention to do so and create a game plan that helps you move to a place that is agreeable to you.

Give yourself permission to explore possibilities and don't worry about the barriers. Far too many people end up rejecting opportunities because they place artificial barriers and idiotic notions of responsibility upon themselves. Don't be one of them. Suffering and being miserable is a habit. There is no need for you to deny yourself the good things in life due to a misguided sense of responsibility.

Ultimately, the person that matters the most is you. I mean, if you're not at your best and happiest, you are of no use to anyone. So prioritize yourself and your well-being and recognize how important you are.

COMMIT

As I mentioned earlier, writing is a powerful act. Take this time to write down all the things you have decided and the habits you will practice that will push you toward your goals. Write down preliminary plans to change your environment for the better and list the actions you think you can do better or new ones that you can take.

Write down your fears as well as every single thing you love about your life. It could be something as simple as looking at the stars at night or smelling freshly baked bread as you walk to work in the morning. Do not underestimate anything!

If you can, create a tentative plan with timelines. Remember, the timeline isn't the point. Your goals and your positive state of mind, matter the most. Recognize that timelines can change as can goals. This is perfectly fine and in fact, indicates growth.

3

WHAT IS FIRE? FINANCIAL
INDEPENDENCE - RETIRE EARLY

*Y*ou might have been wondering why on earth is this book titled *FIRE*? Well, now you know! Financial independence is what we're all here for so let's begin by learning about how to achieve this. Common media on financial independence advises you to set aside money every month and then pray that everything goes well at the end of it all.

As you've seen, the numbers don't back this claim up. If anything, this sort of advice puts you in an even worse position than before. There are many elements to FIRE so in this chapter, you will learn some basic principles of achieving financial independence and also some tips and tools on how to identify the stage you're currently in and what the journey ahead looks like.

The Principles of FIRE

There are four basic principles you need to adhere to so you can retire early. When I say retire early, I'm not talking about quitting your job and sitting around doing nothing. I'm talking about reaching a stage where you don't need your job anymore since your expenses and wants are all taken care of. In other words, you can work when you want to.

Let's dive right into the first principle. This might seem like common advice but is actually misunderstood by a lot of people.

Minimize Expenses

The moment the subject of expenses comes up, the first thing common financial media recommends is to skip that Starbucks latte in the morning or to wave goodbye to your avocado toast. They'd rather have you munching Dr. Kellogg's suppressing cereal or some other piece of cardboard. Somehow, you're supposed to believe that living like this is good for you.

Here's the thing about expenses: You need to minimize them, not eliminate or reduce them. Minimization is a very different mindset from elimination. Technically speaking, I can eliminate expenses by not eating any food. How well is that going to work out? All expenses can be categorized under two broad umbrellas: Needs and wants.

YOUR NEEDS ARE staple expenses that you have to spend.

These are:

- Cost of housing (a mortgage or rent)
- Cost of utilities
- Cost of transport (car+fuel, public transport, car payments)
- Food and water
- Clothes (making sure you have some)
- Maintenance (home, vehicle etc)
- Expenses related to children if you have any (before-and-after school programs, activities, daycare, school tuition, clothes, shoes etc.)
- Home staples (such as cleaning supplies, laundry supplies, kitchen supplies etc.)

That's pretty much it. Needs can never be eliminated

and neither should you eliminate them. The thing about needs is that they can be minimized to a certain extent but beyond a certain point, it's just not worth it. Coupons are a great example of this with regard to grocery shopping.

There's no doubt that using coupons will save you a ton of money. Let's say it takes you a couple hours everyday to search for and collect coupons that save you $800 on your monthly grocery bill. These are substantial savings indeed. How much are those couple hours everyday worth though? You're spending 60 hours per month and are effectively earning $800 at that time (as savings).

What if you could earn more money during those 60 hours. Let's say you manage to find a job that pays you $20 per hour and you manage to work this job for those two hours. You're now earning $1,200 from those two hours instead of just $800. That's a 50% increase!

My point is that it is always better to adopt the viewpoint that making more money is preferable to reducing expenses and trying to squeeze more out of your budget. Instead of trying to confine yourself to living within a small area, why not simply expand the boundaries of that area?

There is a risk/reward element to the time you spend trying to save money. As long as there are no other alternatives, you should seek to minimize the cost of your needs. Understand that you can reduce them to a certain extent. Go below this point and you run the risk of harming yourself. For example, you could buy lower quality food but is it really worth doing this?

The things you can minimize greatly are your wants. Examples of these are:

- Vehicle (a Porsche instead of a used Honda)
- Clothes (Gucci instead of the Gap)
- Food (Whole Foods certified organic instead of Trader Joe's)
- Travel (Tulum instead of Florida)
- Living situation (Downtown loft instead of a suburban apartment or home)
- Home decor (Restoration Hardware instead of Ikea)

Truth be told, there is no end to your wants. My point is that these are the ones you can minimize the most. However, most people take it to an extreme and eliminate them entirely. Your wants are also the target of most financial advice when it comes to budgeting.

Here's the thing: Money exists to be spent or grown. It is useless when it simply sits in your bank doing nothing. Your wants are the things that give you joy when you spend money on them. The key is to figure out which of your wants bring you the most satisfaction and peace of mind, as opposed to the ones that are a reflection of your consumerist desire to spend money.

Most Americans, especially the middle class, are conditioned to want things simply because the media tells them so. Everyone wants to fly to Coachella because that's what the no-talent Instagram influencers are telling them to do. Sure, it's fine if you want to experience it once in your lifetime but unless you really derive happiness or joy from it, eliminate it.

That avocado toast might cost you $10 everyday but as long as you can afford it while hitting your savings goals (more about this in the next chapter), and as long as it ensures a great start to your day, why not indulge yourself? Budgeting and saving is not an exercise in denying things to yourself.

It's about figuring out what brings you the most joy and prioritizing that, while minimizing or eliminating everything else. Keep this in mind as you read the rest of this book.

Leverage... *Not Debt*

To the financially unsavvy crowd, leverage and debt mean the same thing. However, you're not one of them because you're reading this book and I'm here to tell you that there's a world of difference between the two.

It all comes down to assets. Leverage (or smart debt if you will) creates assets for you.

Debt simply burdens you. The distinction gets confusing because most people don't understand what an asset is. In a nutshell, an asset is something that makes you money over the long term. There are two ways an asset can make you money: capital gains and cash flow. For example, a home purchase can make you money when it increases in value and via rental income that you can collect on it, should you decide to rent out a room or two, or the whole place.

The thing with capital gains is that they're unrealized for the most part. In other words, they're on paper until the time comes to sell and aren't cash in hand. Cash flow, as the name suggests is the opposite. You want to prioritize them both equally when investing in an asset. For example, if you draw a mortgage and live in the property, you're prioritizing capital gains entirely. After all, you can't rent the place out if you're occupying it fully.

The American dream storyline gets people to prioritize capital gains at the cost of cash flow. This was fine in the 1960s when everything was rising. However, how do you think people who bought homes in 2005 fared? These people ended up owing more money on their mortgage than their homes were worth! The thing with capital gains is that they're likely to turn into capital losses as well.

This is why cash flow is just as important. Business owners understand this innately. When running a business, cash flow is far more important than capital gains, which largely take care of themselves. The cash balance in the bank is what enables a business to move forward.

I'll address cash flow in greater detail shortly but for now, remember that an asset has to create both cash flow and capital gains to qualify as one. Anything else is just a liability. Loans that finance an asset are leverage and this is a smart thing to do. Loans that don't do so are debt and should be avoided.

Let's look at an example. An 18 year old college kid is considering borrowing $80,000 to fund his undergraduate degree in engineering. He's attending a mediocre school and his job prospects are iffy upon graduation. He can potentially earn a salary of $50,000 per year before taxes but he needs to get a job first. As such, this scenario is leaning towards debt instead of leverage. However, let's say he is attending a prestigious school with a strong engineering program and his chances of securing a $50,000 job are pretty good. In this case, the loan is leverage and is fully worth it.

Real world scenarios are more complex but I'm trying to illustrate how the nature of loans can change depending on the reward side of the equation. The same loan can function as both leverage and debt depending on the situation. Look at both sides of the coin when evaluating choices.

A lot of people pedantically dismiss all loans or borrowed money as being bad. This is a shortsighted thing to do, even if it is the conservative play. The problem is that you'll miss out on huge opportunities to grow your net worth by doing this. So remember: Leverage. Not debt.

INVEST WISELY

The stock market is a great tool to boost your net worth. Like anything else though, it is a tool. You can use a lawnmower to create a perfect turf of grass or you can use it to trim your hedges and end up with a twig in your eye. It depends on your skill. If you happen to be a hedge fund manager or a skilled business person then an appropriate use of the stock market is to pick individual stocks and bet on businesses.

However, for most of us, the safe play is to invest into so called index funds and Exchange Traded Funds or ETFs. These funds seek to capture broad market movement. Mind you, there are many different indices out there. For example, you can invest in the broad stock market index such as the S&P 500 or you can invest in a sector specific index such as the energy or tech sector indices.

The best thing to do is to invest in the broad market index. Historically, these have yielded 8% per year and by purchasing a low cost index fund (for example from Fidelity or Vanguard), you can capture these gains. Keep in mind that these will be capital gains for the most part. However, given the stability of America as a place of doing business and opportunity, you're likely to see an upward push over the long term.

The other investment vehicle you should consider is a Real Estate Investment Trust or REIT (pronounced 'reet'). I'll dive into greater detail in later chapters. For now, forget about trying to day trade or trade options and all that fancy stuff.

In addition to investing in the markets, there are two more things you should do. The first is to invest in yourself by learning new skills and reading more. Hopefully, I don't need to explain why this is a good idea. Second, you should set aside some portion of your income as a potential investment in a passive income business.

The internet has the ability to help you create such businesses. For example, a blog requires initial work and takes time to monetize but eventually, you could earn ad dollars from it by simply maintaining your content. Affiliate marketing and Kindle self publishing are examples of businesses that provide largely passive income once you invest your money in them.

Of course, these require you to do research and invest in courses to learn how to run them properly. Given the largely passive nature of income though, it's worth the investment. You'll earn money while you sleep and there's nothing wrong with that!

PRIORITIZE *Cash Flow*

You could have a stock portfolio with unrealized gains of $1 million but if you have just $5 in the bank, all those gains aren't going to do you much good, are they? Cash is terribly undervalued by most people and this is why they fail to reach financial independence.

Assets that generate cash are invaluable since you can create a wealth snowball that will dramatically increase your net worth. This is why investing in, and creating businesses that generate passive income is so important. The cash that is generated by them can be used to invest in other opportunities and your initial investment multiplies exponentially.

Traditional advice to invest in the stock market exists because it follows the "wait until you retire" narrative. You've already seen how that works out. This doesn't mean you should ignore capital gains heavy assets, instead, you need to maintain a balance between cash flow and capital gains. Whenever you consider an investment opportunity, remember to look at both qualities.

A good idea is to take a look at your investments on the portfolio level. For example, you could have equal amounts of money invested in a broad market index fund (cap gains) and an affiliate marketing business (cash flow). Remember that an asset that is capital gains heavy is a risky prospect for the long term, unless it happens to be backed by extremely strong factors (like index funds are).

On the other hand, an asset that generates 100% cash flow is an extremely safe bet. After all, you can use that cash to create even more assets and capital gains elsewhere. The bottom line is: Aim to maximize your cash flow with all of your opportunities because it creates more cash and capital gains for you.

THE STAGES

There are three stages that you will experience in your journey toward financial independence. These are: survival, security, and independence.

SURVIVAL

Everyone, even the richest people in the world who may be born with silver spoons in their mouths, start off here. We begin our lives completely dependent on our parents for everything. People who have close to no income and need to borrow money or favors from other people in order to merely survive are in this stage.

As you begin to transition out of this stage, you'll see your income levels rise and you'll slowly be able to meet your expenses, even if you struggle to make ends meet and have high levels of debt. People in this stage are marked by their inability to pay for any emergency by themselves.

The highest level people in this stage hit before moving out of it is a state where they're earning more than their expenses and are managing to save some money every month. This is when they begin to save for a rainy day and set aside some money for future investments or begin to work toward reducing their debt levels. At this stage, you are no longer living paycheck to paycheck.

SECURITY

The entry into the second stage is marked by the presence of a rainy day fund. Typically, this is an amount equal to six months' living expenses after taxes. This amount pays for your expenses but not an emergency. As your income levels rise, you will set aside some cash to cover emergencies as well as potential investments.

If you have debt, you will begin to work to reduce the principal on these loans or seek to consolidate your debt into manageable levels. You're no longer looking over your shoulder to see if you can make ends meet and will begin to think about ways of growing your money and net worth. Your income stream is stable and you'll seek to create more streams while increasing your primary source of money.

As you begin to leave this stage, you will reduce or completely eliminate debt and your savings will see a massive jump because of this. You will invest your money into different revenue streams that can generate more income for you. You'll begin to see the fruits of these investments as well in terms of capital gains and cash flow.

Your income levels will continue to increase exponentially as you keep investing in more assets and keep increasing your primary source of income.

INDEPENDENCE

The marker of entering the independence stage is when you are generating enough income from secondary sources to cover your living expenses. In other words, you don't need to work anymore since your investments are paying for your living costs. As your income increases, you will not only manage to cover your expenses but actually save enough money from secondary sources.

Your wealth snowball is well and truly underway and at this point, you can realistically quit your job and do whatever you want. Mind you, it isn't necessarily true that you will have hit your desired level of financial independence, but you'll get there during the later levels of this stage.

The bad news is that most people never get to this level. The good news is that by reading this book, you're putting yourself in a prime position to ensure that you get here!

4

WHAT IS YOUR NUMBER?

I've been going on about savings and how you need to increase your income and so on for a bit now. How much do you need to save anyway? What are the metrics you should use to determine this number and how does it impact your financial independence goals?

In addition to this, I'm going to wade deeper into the debate about cutting spending versus increasing income and which option is better. I've stated my preference previously but it's not as clear cut as you might think. Lastly, you're going to learn about a very interesting study that will simplify any doubts you may have about how much you really need to save for independence and will make the question of retirement math a whole lot simpler.

. . .

YOUR SAVINGS RATE

The average American household saves 10% of their income as I've mentioned before. While this is the average rate, to be brutally honest, this is a pathetic savings rate. As we've seen from the first chapter, the median household income is around $50,000. This means the average American household is saving just $5,000 per year.

The fact is that there is just one major factor that determines how quickly you can reach a stage where you can retire. This is your savings rate. The savings rate itself depends on the amount of money you spend in expenses and the amount of money you earn. I'll be looking at these in more detail shortly.

For now, let us run some simple numbers. Let's assume you're currently earning enough money to pay for all of your living expenses and wants. I understand this might not necessarily be the case but this is for simplicity's sake. We're building a model just like we did in the first chapter in order to understand savings better.

Here are a few assumptions I'm making:

- You earn 5% on your nest egg/savings in perpetuity
- You withdraw just 4% of it to pay for your expenses

- Your expenses remain at the same level as what they are right now

Running the numbers gives us some interesting figures. For starters, we can realize that a 10% savings rate will require us to work for 51 years in order to be able to retire and save enough to replace our income. If you save 20%, you can replace your income in 37 years. If you want to retire in 10 years, you need to save 65% of your income.

If you manage to save half of your income, you can replace your current income in 17 years.

Isn't That Unrealistic?

One of the conclusions you will reach after looking at those numbers is that they seem far out of reach. After all, how realistic is it to live on just 35% of your income, after taxes? Let's say you earn $50,000 after taxes. This means you need to live on $17,500 per year or $1,458 per month.

This might be achievable in rural areas but it isn't a realistic budget in a place such as New York City. Keep in mind is that there is a trade off between your location and earning ability. While the cost of living in rural or less crowded areas is low, your ability to earn higher levels of income is reduced as well.

The real killer is if you live in a high income area but earn less than the average wage. For example, someone earning $50,000 in New York City is in a less than optimal situation than someone who earns $100,000 who lives in Salt Lake City, UT.

Having said that, aiming to live on half of your income after taxes should be your goal. The key is to identify what your situation is like and what you need to do to achieve this number. There are qualitative aspects to this as well. Everyone needs a certain level of comfort to function at their best. For example, the needs of a 40 year old will be more expensive than those of 21 year old. This is just how life works.

There are two sides to the equation. The first is the amount of money you spend and the other is how much you make. As I've mentioned earlier, you should seek to prioritize both, leaning on the side of making more money or increasing your income as much as you can.

I'll get into this in more detail but for now, understand that the math behind figuring out how much you need to save before you can realistically consider retirement is pretty straight forward. If you wish to quit your job in 10 years time, you need to save at least 65% of your income.

This requires you to sacrifice a lot of things that others might take for granted. It might require you to cook more food at home and cut out eating out at restaurants or ordering takeout completely. You might have to drive a beater of a Honda instead of leasing that sweet Tesla, like your friends do. You might have to opt to buy clothes when they go on sale instead of buying them off the rack at full price.

It comes down to what your priorities are and what's important to you. I'm not saying you need to punish yourself to achieve that magical 50% savings figure. Instead, you need to perform a ground reality check on your lifestyle and see what you need to do. Everyone has different needs. Person A might not prioritize good clothing or food but this might be a need for Person B. This is fine.

Take stock of what your reality is and then figure out how to get to 50% savings.

CUTTING EXPENSES OR INCREASING INCOME?

As I mentioned earlier, there are two ways for you to increase your savings. Obviously, you will want to do both but there comes a point where you will need to prioritize one over the other. Both options have their own advantages and disadvantages.

I have mentioned my preference for increasing income over cutting expenses but there are some very credible voices who advocate prioritizing cutting expenses. At the end of the day, it comes down to how you view this debate and what makes the most sense for you. You might find that my arguments don't work for you and that cutting expenses is more realistic for you to pursue.

My objective is to lay out both sides of the argument so that you can make an informed choice. Let's begin by assessing how much we can maximize our savings when we cut our expenses. There is a powerful fact inherent in the act of cutting your expenses. First, this automatically puts money in your pocket. Second, it reduces your need to spend money on that item for the rest of your life thereby creating a veritable income stream for you.

Lastly, there is a psychological fact at work as well. This is because as income levels increase, so do your expenses. This is just normal human nature and it is pretty difficult to control. This is not to say that you should never seek to increase income. It's just that prioritizing it might inadvertently lead you to increase your expenses as well.

That being said, there are some downsides to prioritizing the reduction of expenses over everything else. For starters, it forces you to look at things in a negative manner. In other words, you'll have to constantly ask yourself "What can I do without?" The aim of achieving financial independence isn't to just stop going to work;

It's to be able to afford a lifestyle where you'll be able to cater to your wants as well as needs.

This doesn't mean that everyone is looking to spend a million dollars a month living the high life. However, adopting an attitude of cutting costs gets you focused on just the costs and you'll end up incurring the biggest cost of them all: the cost of opportunity.

I mentioned an example previously where you spend a couple of hours searching for and collecting coupons to reduce your grocery bill and how this time investment only makes sense if you were saving more doing this than what you could earn by working during these two hours. Let's say you could earn $1,20 but saved just $80.

If you choose to continue saving, your opportunity cost is -$40. This is a simple example but in real life, opportunity costs are harder to estimate. Let's say you could spend those two hours researching a new online business opportunity that could one day make you $5,000 per month within ten months' time. What's the opportunity cost here?

There's also the question of freedom and what it truly means. Does freedom mean reducing your spending to just bare-bones necessities or is it having the ability to be able to buy that Starbucks latte because it makes you feel good, expenses and logic be damned? Most people save money to be able to enjoy things like that latte and not to look at their bank balances and pat themselves on the back.

Yes, it's great to be able to retire before the age of 30 by cutting expenses, but ask yourself which of the following choices seem better to you:

- You're financially independent but need to severely restrict your spending on things like fancy food and holidays to once a month to once a quarter.
- You're not independent and have a decent level of savings but can buy that latte without thinking twice about it.

My guess is most people would choose the latter. The intense focus on the negatives (expenses) will usually end up costing you opportunities. Most people don't realize this because there's no cash cost to opportunities.

This is one of the big advantages of minimizing costs as much as possible but ultimately focusing on building your income streams. In an ideal world, if you could build your income streams enough, you can stop worrying about costs altogether. This isn't a practical situation but it does highlight how much better things can be.

Focusing on building income streams will have you

working toward true independence. In other words, it forces you to think of the return on your time investment. Is it worth pursuing a side hustle that will make you $20 per hour but requires four hours work everyday or a passive business that can make you $10 per hour but requires less than ten minutes work everyday?

A business oriented mindset is at the heart of prioritizing your income streams and this is intimidating to most people. You see, to truly maximize your income, you're going to have to build a passive income stream. This requires you to invest time upfront and trust that the rewards will present themselves. Most people don't think of themselves as being business oriented and pick the safe option that is reducing expenses.

This is a shortsighted approach. It's a bit like saying the FIRE method is too tough and therefore adopting the old approach of investing a few nibbles here and there in a 401(k) is the best way forward. It is challenging to build a business and yes, you will likely lose some money as you build your business. However, the rewards are well worth it.

Besides, the internet has democratized information to such an extent that running a location-independent online business is not such a far fetched thought. There are tons of business models out there for you to get started with. It's not like the old days where you need to open a brick and mortar store and sit in it all day waiting for people to walk in.

The risk is that none of your ventures might work and you'll end up with a less than optimal amount of savings in the end. This is why prudently investing only money you can afford to lose is crucial. What I mean is that you should not invest your entire savings into a business venture upfront. I'll discuss this in more detail in a later chapter.

For now, read through this section again and see which viewpoint appeals to you more. Remember that this isn't an all or nothing choice. We're only talking about a marginal prioritization here. Someone who seeks to maximize income streams is also minimizing costs. It's a shift in mindset that we're talking about at the end of the day.

How Much Do You Need?

One of the most basic questions that people have is: "How much do I need to retire?" This is a good question and for the longest time, there wasn't a definitive answer. The short answer is, you multiply your annual expenses by 25 and this is the principal you can retire with.

The long answer involves a bunch of assumptions and a bit of history. It all begins with assuming how much you need to live comfortably. This is why we begin with how much you will realistically spend every year. Note that this amount isn't the same as what you're currently spending. It is the amount you would like to spend so you can lead your ideal lifestyle.

As I said, not everyone wants to live like a high roller all the time. For example, if you wish to split time living somewhere in Southeast Asia and North America, you're looking at an average monthly cost of around $3000 (this is a high level estimate of course). This means your yearly expenses will be $36,000. Multiply this by 25 and you get $900,000.

Let's not focus on the size of the principal for now. Where does the 25 come from? We multiply by this number because we're assuming that your expenses will be four percent of your overall principal (900000*.04 = 36000.) In other words, you'll withdraw four percent of your principal every year to pay for your expenses.

Assuming your principal doesn't grow, this amount will last you 25 years. This isn't good enough since we want this to last in perpetuity. To counter this, we're assuming that the principal is invested in a place that provides a seven percent average annual return.

Inflation is assumed to take three percent of this so you're left with four percent at the end of the day and your principal thus remains the same. Remember that this is just a model and in the real world, the numbers won't work out this smoothly. The reason four percent is assumed to be a safe withdrawal rate is thanks to an academic study called the *Trinity Study*.

The aim of the research conducted was to determine what an ideal withdrawal rate would be for the average American given the gyrations of the stock markets over the years and other factors such as interest rates and so on. It turns out that four percent was the lowest and thus safest withdrawal rate that people can get away with over time. During some periods of American history, you could have withdrawn eight percent and still have enough left over.

I must mention that there are a few reasonable criticisms of the Trinity study. For starters, it covers a relatively short period of American economic history, even if the study extended from the 1900s till 2000. Compared to an entire body of economic factors that have occurred, 100 years doesn't rate much.

Those 100 years are also quite exceptional in world history. They happen to contain the rise of America as the preeminent power in the world and possibly the longest bull run the financial markets have ever seen, occasional economic crashes and crises notwithstanding. Consider this, in 1900, America firmly stood behind European powers such as Britain, France, Germany, and Russia in terms of economic might. By the end of that period, there was no nation that could match it.

No other country in the world has had such a run of success ever. The only comparable nation is Germany under Bismarck when it transformed from an economy rooted in agriculture to a bonafide world power. That run lasted between 25 to 30 years. Thus, the Trinity study is hobbled by too much prosperity it would seem.

Next, there's no way to tell what the next 100 years will look like, irrespective of how many years you study. I mean, only psychics can predict the future and even they get it wrong sometimes. So how should you approach all of this? How can you ensure that you manage to land in the ballpark where the 4% withdrawal rate is enough or is a decent estimate?

Margin of Safety

When he was once asked about one of the secrets of his insane wealth, Warren Buffett replied that the principle of the margin of safety was the core of everything he did. The principle itself is quite common across a number of academic fields and in fact, every single one of us applies it instinctively.

Picture this: You're asked to come up with a number that indicates the safest possible following distance between vehicles on a highway where the speed limit is 70MPH. You conduct your research and do a lot of smart calculations because you're intelligent and come up with a time oriented distance of two seconds. In other words, you should be two seconds behind the guy in front of you.

However, is this the number you'll release to the public? After all, your study contains a number of assumptions and models that might not fit the real world 100%. "Better safe than sorry," you tell yourself and release a figure of four seconds. In essence, you double the calculated value and figure that the increase in value will override any assumption errors.

This increase in value is what the margin of safety is. There are many things in our world that are unpredictable and thus we instinctively increase or decrease our estimates when applying calculations to real world situations. For example, engineers double their calculations to account for errors in measurements and estimation. Sensible people add a 'miscellaneous' line item to the budgets to account for expenses that they cannot foresee.

The margin of safety brings us back to our original consideration of how much of your income you should save. Living on half of your income or working as much as possible to get to this figure, means applying a margin of safety to your calculations so you can have enough breathing room in case you've estimated some-thing incorrectly, or if you will need to increase your spending down the road.

Build a margin of safety into all of your financial considerations. I'm not saying you should assume the worst every single time. Just don't assume things will turn out for the best every single time. This might sound pessimistic but there's a difference between constant pessimism and defensive pessimism. The latter helps make sure you've dotted every 'i' and cross every 't' and will keep you on the right side of all of your retirement calculations.

5

GETTING YOUR EXPENSES UNDER CONTROL

*B*udgeting. There, I said it. I can see you yawning back there but understand that the very basis of your ability to become financially independent rests on how well and realistically you can budget your expenses.

The thing about expenses is that they come in different forms. Some of them come in a big lump sum, while some steadily chip away at your money. It can be tough to understand the nature of all of your expenses and map them out properly. By the end of this chapter, this is not going to be a problem anymore.

The Basics of Budgeting

Creating a budget is more than just typing in the names of a few expenses in an excel file and allocating maximum spending amounts to them. Before you do that, you need to think of your money in a different way. Those line items in a budget (food, rent, car payments etc.) aren't just words. They're tasks that your money needs to fulfill.

Every dollar that comes into your bank account has a job to do. Your monthly income has to perform certain duties. The advantage of thinking in this manner is to get you used to thinking that your money is working for you and that you're the master. A lot of people are slaves to their money when really, it's the other way around. So take charge of your finances and make it work for you instead!

Once you've decided that your income fulfills a job requirement, the next step is to understand that you are a money manager. Money managers are usually thought of as being people who run millions of dollars in the financial markets and have huge investors backing them. Well, this is not that case. If you have money in the bank, it needs to be managed and directed to perform its job.

Most people don't think of themselves as being money managers and instead adopt a reactive approach to their money. They plan their expenses and spend it as soon as cash arrives into their account, instead of proactively looking at expenses versus income. One of the things you'll need to do as a money manager is to get used to handling overflows.

By overflow, I mean a situation where you'll exceed the budget limit of a line item. Say you allocated $300 for groceries this month but exceeded it by $50. Well, if you spent $50 less on entertainment, then they offset one another. Get used to moving money around categories like this and you'll become more comfortable with it.

Lastly, understand the concept of "gain money." What I mean is that you need to have enough money in the bank to pay for an entire month's worth of expenses at the start of the month. It takes time to build up to this but by following the tips in this chapter, you'll get there within a few months.

Let's now take a look at the individual line items in your budget.

. . .

BUDGET CATEGORIES

Creating a budget list is simple enough. Here are the most common line items:

1. Rent/Mortgage
2. Utilities
3. Groceries
4. Gym/exercise classes
5. Health expenses/Medical expenses
6. Vehicle/Transport costs
7. Entertainment (going out etc.)
8. Insurance payments
9. Debt payments if any
10. Miscellaneous costs

Your own list will vary depending on your situation. When creating this list, a common stumbling block is the issue of one-time payments and how to handle them. Usually, they occur just once or twice a year and when they do, everything gets thrown out of whack since they blow up expenses spectacularly. As a result, your cash projections will fluctuate accordingly.

The best way to handle them is to amortize them. Amortization is an accounting concept where a single lump sum is broken down into smaller payments and the cost of it is booked every month. Say you have a large payment of $5,000 coming up in six months time.

Create a line item that adequately names it and account for it every month by dividing 5,000 by six.

Thus, every month, you'll record an expense of $833.30 in your budget and this money will be set aside in your account.

These days, the best way to maintain and create a budget is to use software such as Mint or Youneed-abudget.com. These apps connect to your bank account directly through secure and encrypted servers, and give you the ability to run reports on your spending patterns to see what you can cut down on and the things you're spending too much money on.

When looking to minimize your spending, remember to identify and get clear on your needs and wants. You can eliminate wants completely but this would lead to a very dull existence indeed. One of the best ways to gain the mindset of you being the master of your money is to use it on things that you enjoy doing or really look forward to doing.

Let's say you love having a slice of blueberry pie at the luxurious bakery downtown. Why not set aside some money every week or every month (depending on your situation) and go ahead and spend that money? You can label it "celebration money" or "date night money" or whatever you like.

Using your money this way enforces discipline over

your wants and also reinforces that your money is there to serve your needs. It could be something as simple as buying a $5 candy bar once a month. If you derive satisfaction from it, do it. I must make a note here of habits that can turn into addictions such as smoking or drinking.

Whether you choose to pursue these is entirely up to you. This isn't the kind of book where I'm going to ask you to quit smoking or else you'll get cancer etc. I mean, you are an adult after all. However, do take a look at your expenses in this area and see if you can reduce them. Often, the amount of money people spend on tobacco amounts to much more than what they spend on food. Minimizing and regaining control over this is a good way to curb your spending.

Lastly, adopting a minimalist lifestyle and reducing clutter goes a long way toward minimizing expenses. If you do have a lot of stuff lying around your home, you can even sell these items and earn some pocket money. Clutter only increases the number of things you need to take care of. By minimizing this, you'll automatically increase the number of things in your life that you truly value and care about.

While the budget line items largely sort themselves out, the underlying question you should ask yourself is how to divide the money that's entering your account.

. . .

An important part of budgeting is to decide on the ideal proportion of income you wish to divide between expenses and savings. As mentioned earlier, you should be saving at least 50% of your income ideally. This 50% ought to be divided in a 40/10 split where 40% goes towards general savings and the other 10% goes towards setting up a passive business opportunity. In other words, this is your capital that you will begin accumulating.

Of the remaining 50% of your income, 40% should be directed towards expenses and the remaining 10% should be directed toward investing in yourself. This can be done by learning new skills, a new language or buying books and courses that improve your overall lifestyle and wellbeing.

There are two exceptions to this division of your income. The first is when you're just starting out trying to manage your money. Before you begin dividing your money in these proportions, your priority should be to accumulate at least seven months' worth of living expenses after taxes.

So if you spend $1,500 per month in living expenses, you should spend 40% of your total income paying for your expenses and the remaining 60% needs to be directed towards accumulating $10,500 ($1,500*7 months.) Once you've accumulated this amount, you need to set aside some money as an emergency fund. This amount varies for everyone and can be used to pay for anything unforeseen such as a sudden expense related to your home or your car and so on.

Your emergency cash and six (not seven) months living expenses should be held in a high yield savings account where it will earn some level of interest. When placing it in those accounts, make sure there are no withdrawal limits of any kind. You can keep one months' worth of living expenses in your checking account and use this to pay for the upcoming month's expenses. Thus, you'll age your money by a month.

Only after all this is done should you start investing in yourself and setting aside 10% of your income toward a potential business venture. Your employer might offer a 401(k) plan with matching benefits. You should take advantage of this or of any pre-tax investment benefits. You can include these amounts as a part of your 40% savings allocation or consider just the after tax portion of your income for division, it's up to you.

The second scenario where these divisions won't matter is when your income simply isn't large enough to divide in this manner. For example, if you're earning $1,000 per month and need to spend $700 on living expenses, the proportions suggested above are unrealistic to say the least.

In such situations, you should direct your savings

toward accumulating a seven month buffer and an emergency store of cash. You might think that this will take forever but this assumes you'll never increase your income. There's no other way of saying this but you'll need to find ways to increase your income by devoting more time to work. Do whatever it takes, whether it be holding down a second job or providing some sort of service in your spare time.

People in such situations tend to downplay the importance of their wants. The truth is that while you should be reducing your wants as much as possible, you should not eliminate them completely. Life is tough but there's no need to punish yourself. Look at indulging the smallest want you have. Like in the example of the $5 candy bar that satisfies you, look to indulge in the little things that bring you pleasure.

If you really don't want to spend any money, then at the very least travel to places that are 'rich' in nature. Go sit in the lobby of a fancy hotel or go visit a mall that has a bunch of luxury stores. Just because you have a low income now doesn't mean this will always be the case. Trust the process.

Once you've accumulated enough money for your buffer amounts, you need to start putting your savings into a high yield account where it can earn some interest. Now comes the critical bit: You should look at increasing your skills and use the money in savings to do this. Essentially, use the rest of your money as an education fund which will increase your income. You are your biggest asset, so invest in yourself and your skills.

The reason you should do this is because there's no point saving paltry amounts of money in a savings account. Savings accounts, even high yield ones, yield just two percent on average. There's no way you'll become financially independent by doing this. Increase your skills and invest your time in ventures that will potentially increase your income down the road.

Buy courses, attend classes, and always seek to increase your income. Don't worry about investing in the stock market at this point. Until you're at a stage where the proportions suggested earlier make sense, stay away from it. Don't try to speculate in the markets by day trading or trading options and futures either. You need money you can afford to lose to do this and you have none right now.

You might not see it a this point but all of these experiences are making you an excellent money manager. After all, the more money you have, the less you need to juggle it around. You're building your skills in these areas and as your income grows, you're only going to allocate it more efficiently. So ride these rough times out and use your money to make yourself feel good, as much as you possibly can.

Some examples of minimizing expenses are to use a bike to travel if this makes sense. This way, you'll get your share of exercise and will eliminate an expensive car payment and insurance. If you do need a car, get one that doesn't need a monthly payment and isn't a gas guzzler. Another option is to cancel all cable subscriptions and rely on phone data plans to use the internet. This depends on the area you live in, of course.

In some places, cable operators do not unbundle internet and cable subscriptions so in this case, using a phone-only plan might make the most sense. The point is to prioritize spending money on things that really benefit you as opposed to providing you with temporary relief. Sure, the season finale of your favorite show might be on right now but it is really worth paying $100 for a cable subscription to watch it?

Tips to Reduce Expenses

Everybody could use a few tips with regards to expenses. Here are a few that will help you save more cash.

Shop Around

This one's a no-brainer. Always shop around for deals

before purchasing anything. Whether it be car insurance, health insurance or gym memberships, always take a look at your various options. Gym memberships are currently being disrupted, as the folks out in Silicon Valley like to say.

The rise of services such as Class Pass are changing the dynamic of gym pricing. It might be worth it to sign up for services such as these and have a greater variety of services than restrict yourself to a single big box gym.

Groom *Smartly*

This one is far easier for men to implement than it is for women I'll admit. All men need to do is wear clothes that fit them well, shine their shoes, and get a clean haircut. Admittedly, most of us men fail at this but that's a different subject. Women tend to have far more expenses in this regard but either way, look to minimize your expenses here.

Trying out a few home remedies might be in order instead of spending all that money at a salon. For the men reading this, minimizing any clothing or grooming expenses does not mean you have a free pass to look like a caveman. It doesn't cost much to dress well and look presentable so don't ignore this.

· · ·

Learn to Cook

This single tip will save you more money and improve your health. By cooking at home, you'll have full control over what you eat and you'll stop donating money to restaurants. If cooking intimidates you, watch some videos on Youtube and learn how to make some simple dishes. Your stomach and wallet will thank you for it.

Entertain Yourself Smartly

Everything is smart these days, from phones to TVs to ovens. Why not be smart in your entertainment choices? Choose services that you can pay for as you go or ones that allow you to minimize your bills. Do you really need to drink alcohol every time you go out or is it possible for you to have a good time without it? Can you reduce the number of cigarettes you smoke?

Run the numbers on everything and see what works. Always look to make your entertainment more efficient.

Location Arbitrage

This one is not a common thing to do and it might not work for most. However, for those that it does work for, it's golden. What is the cost to rent an average one bedroom apartment in Manhattan per month? My guess is it's going to be around $3,500 to $5000. This is just rent, of course.

Add in living expenses and you're looking at spending around $6,500 per month if you want to live like a decent human being. What would be the cost of a similar lifestyle in Kuala Lumpur, Malaysia? Or in one of Bali's beachside towns? Or in Buenos Aires, Argentina? Glad you asked! The costs are $900, $1,500, and $1,300 respectively.

Earning in US dollars and spending in a currency of lesser value has been an open secret of the digital nomad community for a long time now. There are just two things that stop people from realizing this reality. The first is the lack of a location independent job or business, the other is fear of relocating or moving away from loved ones.

This is why I'm stressing the importance of creating a passive business. Not only will you make more money, you'll end up saving more thanks to lesser costs. Best of all, you'll live a lifestyle that compares very well to the one back home and in many cases will be even better. I mean, $6,000 goes much further in Bali than it does in New York.

The second thing that stops people from realizing this reality is just plain old ignorance. Most Americans probably have no idea where Kuala Lumpur is, let alone know that its infrastructure is better than most American cities along with it being one of the most cosmopolitan cities in the world (translation: Everyone speaks English.)

Happily, all it takes to rectify this is a Google search. This is the true power of the internet. You're not shackled to a single place anymore and the entire world is open to you. So go ahead and explore your options!

6

TRIM THE FAT

*L*et's talk about debt now. Trying to become financially independent while carrying debt is a lot like driving a car with the handbrake on. It doesn't matter how hard you press the accelerator, the vehicle simply won't move very fast. Even worse, keep applying pressure to the accelerator and you'll end up damaging it.

All you can do is release the handbrake before you contemplate moving forward. This is easier said than done when it comes to debt. After all, there are so many varieties of them that it can make your head spin.

This chapter will walk you through the best ways of paying down your debt. Remember that paying down debt should be your number one priority at all times.

. . .

DEBT REDUCTION METHODS

The first rule of eliminating debt is to avoid the thing in the first place. Understandably, this isn't the most practical of scenarios for most people. If you're reading this book, you probably have some form of debt already. If you're someone who's considering taking on debt, I strongly encourage you to review the section previously where I detailed the difference between leverage and debt and evaluate which type you're taking on.

It's time to figure out the best way to reduce your debt. Before you begin to do so, understand that you need to view your debt as being the worst thing that has happened to you. This isn't an exaggeration. The reason I'm mentioning this is because a lot of people have a shockingly casual attitude to their debt.

One reason for this is the high levels of debt that people usually carry. When talking of mountains the size of $100,000, it can be tough to envision how you could ever pay it off. A lot of people work second jobs and seek additional income to pay down debt but only end up spending more and the debt remains untouched for the most part.

So stop viewing your debt as an inconvenience and start viewing it as an emergency. Before you do anything else, you need to eliminate it or bring it down to levels where you can pay off the balances in full every period.

If you're faced with a huge amount of debt that's spread out over multiple sources, here's what you can do.

Consolidation

Debt consolidation should be your first approach. Instead of making several payments to different sources, try to make one payment that goes towards all of them. A lot of times, debt reconsolidation will result with you ending up with a slightly lower payment but this is not guaranteed of course.

Either way, summing your debts together into one payment is a good idea because it helps you get a better handle on what your burden looks like. Too often, multiple payments of $100 on one or two credit cards, $1,500 on a line of credit, and $500 on another loan can cause people to underestimate how much they're really paying.

Credit Card Balances

Credit cards can be weapons of mass destruction in the wrong hands. This is unfortunate because when used wisely, credit cards will actually save you money. To begin with, if you have multiple credit card balances, check whether you can move your balances onto a single card with the lowest interest rate.

Alternatively, see if you qualify for a credit card that has a zero balance transfer fee and zero percent interest. The zero interest usually applies for an introductory period so make sure to check the fine print on how much the rate will be once the promotion period ends. If the interest rate is equal to or lower than the lowest rate you're paying right now, transfer your balances there.

Sometimes, people transfer their balances onto a card that offers great rewards without paying attention to the terms of the promotion and the interest rate that it comes with. This is a result of not treating debt like an emergency. Think of it this way: If the roof of your home was blown away, would you sit around planning a vacation to Bora Bora?

Refinancing

Mortgages on homes that you solely occupy are one of the worst forms of debt because of the huge opportunity costs involved. Not only are you stripping away any chance of cash flow from your asset, you're tying up money into debt, when in fact, it can be used elsewhere. The irony is that people with great credit scores who supposedly are good with money end up in this situation.

Since the housing crisis of the previous decade, a lot of people have found themselves underwater in their mortgages. In other words, they owe more on their mortgage than what their home is worth. These cases are extremely difficult to handle and it is best to consult with a mortgage professional who can advise you on the best course forward since there are so many variables to the situation.

If you aren't underwater, but are still looking to reduce your mortgage burden, look into refinancing your mortgage. Again, just like with credit card debt, beware of promotional rates or floating rates that rise astronomically once the period ends. Some mortgage brokers will convince you that you can "always refinance" but don't fall for this trap.

Truth be told, floating rate mortgages or adjustable rate mortgages can make a lot of sense but given your debt situation, it is inadvisable to add more risk into your financial life. At this point, look to eliminate the burden as much as possible.

PAYMENT STRATEGIES

Once you've worked your way through the above options, you're faced with a choice. If you have multiple debts with different interest rates and payment terms, it can be difficult to decide how to allocate your money to paying off each source of debt. There are two ways you can choose to do this.

The first is called the snowball method and was developed by author Dave Ramsey which advocates paying off your smallest debts first and then working your way upward. The way it works is this. Let's say you owe three principal amounts of $1,500, $2,000, and $18,000 each.

You should seek to make the minimum payments on the $2,000 and $18,000 debts while dedicating as much cash as possible to eliminating the $1,500 debt. In other words, your aim is to make far more than just the minimum payment on that debt. This way, you'll end up eliminating that faster.

Mathematically, this approach doesn't make much sense. However, math is no match for human psychology. Research indicates the people who adopt this style of debt repayment tend to eliminate their debts a lot faster than those who choose to approach the issue mathematically.

The psychological lift that you will receive and the sense of accomplishment you get by looking at your debt balance being reduced will fuel you to work harder towards reducing your burden. Besides, it also offers a nice pat on the back which the other method lacks.

The mathematical way of approaching the situation is called the avalanche method. This method is far more analytical and focuses on the interest rate instead of the principal. Instead of allocating everything you can to the smallest debt principal, you'll be allocating that additional amount to the debt with the highest interest rate.

Using our example, if the $18,000 debt had the highest interest rate, you'll pay the minimum balance on the other debts, but will allocate all additional money to this balance in order to pay it off. The fact is that interest payments will add up massively over time and with average credit card interest rates hovering above 20%, these payments can add up.

Note that the avalanche method is far more cold-blooded and unemotional about the entire repayment process and focuses entirely on the numbers alone. If you're someone who's analytical and is patient, then this method is for you. If you prefer little victories and feel exhausted just looking at your statements, then the snowball method is for you.

There are other methods out there but these two happen to be the most efficient. Your objective with both is to eliminate debt completely and get to a point where you can pay off your entire principal within the loan period instead of making the minimum payments (in the case of credit card debt.)

Vehicles

Let's look at another source of debt in America right now that is created solely out of ignorance. I'm talking about car loans and leases. To be frank, until you achieve financial independence and can afford to throw some money away, you have no business getting into a car lease. This is a lot like renting a car for a longer duration and then giving it back, with a lot less in your pocket.

Lease Vs Loan

There is a lot of literature on this argument. When buying a car, should you lease it or finance it? My contention is that the very premise of this argument is flawed. All lease versus loan arguments compare the cost of leasing to buying a brand new car on loan. The argument eventually arrives at the conclusion that there's a breakeven point where the lease makes more sense and beyond this point, a loan is the better option.

I'm not going to get into this debate and will simply say that it is flawed (you'll learn why shortly). You should not be leasing a car in the beginning. Leases are viewed as being attractive thanks to the fancier cars you can drive for the same price as a loan payment on a much less attractive car.

The holiday season sees a lot of dealerships provide special offers and the chance to impress everyone with your shiny new German sedan. The problem is that the German car isn't yours. You're just renting it. What if someone told you that you can rent a phone for a few years and then will have to return it and get something else for yourself? Or what if someone told you that you need to do the same with your laptop?

Most people would consider this absurd but turn a blind eye towards vehicles. Car lovers are especially guilty of this and it can take a lot of self control to hold yourself back. My suggestion is to save up some money and go blow it on a single day's rental of a luxury vehicle.

Instead of opting to lease a Mercedes, save up and allocate blowing away money (remember this from the chapter on budgeting?) toward renting a Ferrari for a day. You'll get the adrenaline out of your system in a fiscally responsible manner, even if the same can't be said of your driving.

What to Buy

I said the lease versus loan argument is flawed and the

biggest reason is that it presupposes you'll buy a new car. Buying a new car is one of the worst things you can do financially. The minute you buy that shiny new car, it begins to lose value. In effect, what you're doing is taking on a loan where you're underwater right from the start. People would never do this with a house, but for some reason think it's okay to do this with cars.

Some people buy used cars with a loan and this can make sense on some occasions depending on the car model and how much it has depreciated. Depreciation refers to the loss in the car's value. For example, a Toyota Camry on average loses 25% of its value over three years. In other words, it depreciates or has depreciated by that value over three years.

The best way to buy a car is to pay for it in a single payment or pay it off within a year at the most. This means you'll realistically need around $10,000 or so to buy a decent car. Yes, it will be used and yes it will probably have at least 80,000 miles on it. It won't look great and might have been a hot car back when you were in middle school.

If these things bother you, go back and review your 'why.' Why is financial independence important to you and why are these sacrifices necessary? Remind yourself of it every time you look at your car. If it really pains you to drive the thing, start saving up and treat yourself to that one glorious day where you can thrash a Ferrari.

The size of the payment poses a mental block for a lot of people. It is easier to envision yourself paying $350 per month than it is paying $10,000 in a single shot. The thing to do is to check what your total payments amount to instead of looking at them as single payments over time. If you're paying $350 over 48 months, that's $16,500.

Next, look at the sticker price for the car. In all probability, it'll be somewhere around $12,500 or $13,000. This means you're paying an additional $3,500 for the privilege of making smaller payments. Lastly, how much will your car be worth at the end of the loan period? Assuming a 10% depreciation rate, it'll be worth $9,000 or so. This means you're paying $16,500 for something that will be worth $9,000 once you're done with it.

Your loss is $7,500. Why don't you head over to your bank right now, withdraw 7,500 in cash and pay in full or as a down payment? How would you react to someone doing this? You'd probably think they're crazy. Yet, this is what you're signing up for.

The other reason most people don't buy cheap used cars is due to a fear of it breaking down. It's true that car parts begin needing replacement once they go past the 70-80,000 mile mark. However, the cost of parts replacement varies greatly depending on the make of the car.

Japanese cars have ample spare parts available and are quite reliable. This is why they tend to depreciate a lot less than their Korean or American counterparts. The other top tip is to not take your car for servicing to the dealership, which tends to add on a bunch of costs thanks to the relationship they have with the parent brand.

Instead, find a reliable local mechanic by asking your friends and family. You can also visit any auto part stores to find local mechanics who'll have more than enough spare parts for your car and you'll end up paying a lot less for maintenance. Will maintenance cost you as much as depreciation on a new car?

It's impossible to predict how much you'll need to spend exactly but as long as you stick to reliable brands and makes, you'll do just fine.

HOMES

You need a place to live and this spawns a major debate between renting versus owning. The brief answer is that renting has its advantages as does owning. Instead of focusing on these individual terms, you need to think of the question in terms of the return your money earns overall.

Recall what you previously learned about what an asset truly is. If you've taken a loan to finance something that appreciates at a rate of 10% and are paying 4% interest, your gross return is 6%. Instead, if you can invest your principal amount (the loan down payment) into something that pays you 7%, your loan is debt and isn't leverage.

However, if your alternative investment returns less than 6%, your loan is leverage and not debt. It all comes down to how much your money is going to earn. Currently, the average rate of appreciation of home values in America is five percent which is a full two points below the 7% that the broad stock market returns.

So, on the surface, owning a home isn't a great idea. However, there are other factors you need to consider.

WHEN AND HOW TO *Purchase*

Some people have life situations that demand stability. For example, if you have kids you cannot reasonably expect to rent a home forever since you never know when the owner is likely to turn up and ask you to vacate. In such cases, stability concerns trump any fiscal decisions you need to make.

The best thing for most people to do is to delay a home purchase until it is absolutely necessary. The only exception to this is there's such an obviously profitable situation that you'd be foolish to pass up. I'll detail the specifics of such situations in a later chapter. For now, it's best to delay the purchase. When you do purchase a home, it's best to employ a method called house hacking.

House hacking is a new term that has been coined and is attributed to one of the many things millennials have created. The truth is that house hacking is something financially savvy people have been doing for a while since it just makes good sense to do this. The premise is quite simple. You find a property to live in and occupy a portion of it.

You then rent the remaining portion to tenants and collect rents. The idea is to have the rent subsidize your mortgage payment. One of the reasons house hacking is so attractive, apart from the financial sense it makes is that, you will qualify for what is called owner occupied financing.

These loans come with lower interest rates and better terms attached to them. As a result, not only can you rent the remaining property you're buying, you can also lower your mortgage payment thereby making it more likely that it will be covered by the rental income.

By house hacking, you're putting yourself in a position to capture both capital gains as well as cash flow from your investment. In other words, you're leveraging yourself and this is how you should go about borrowing money. To learn more about house hacking you can refer to www.biggerpockets.com or buy the book written on the subject by the founder of *Bigger Pockets*, Craig Curelop.

OTHER OPTIONS

If house hacking does not work for you for whatever reason, it isn't the end of the road. If you live in an area that is close to a tourist spot, you can place it for rent on Airbnb to earn some additional cash flow from it. Make sure your property qualifies to be listed as such since every country has different rules regarding this.

The other option you have is to move to an area that is lower in cost but you don't want to compromise on your quality of life. It is a tough choice to make since this option will have you foregoing cash flow most likely. As such, this should be your worst case scenario so do whatever you can to make house hacking work.

Not only can you live in a decent area by doing this, you will also boost your net worth considerably.

7

WAYS TO INCREASE YOUR INCOME

*T*his is the exciting bit! How would you like to make more money? This chapter is going to walk you through a bunch of ways you can make money both passively and actively. The internet has been a real blessing in terms of making more money as I've mentioned repeatedly in this book.

The most important thing you'll be learning in this chapter is the importance of a different type of leverage along with the various methods you can employ to utilize this principle and make some cash.

TIME AND MONEY

'Time is money," you've been told. I'm not sure who coined that phrase but it's more apt than you can imagine. The thing is that time is the only resource we have that cannot be replenished. This means that the time you spend doing anything that needs to be the most optimal usage of it.

The way you choose to make additional income is crucial when you think of it in terms of time. Even if you are single now without any obligations, at some point in your life you're likely going to start a family, have kids, etc. This means you'll need to be smart about how you manage your time.

If you're going to spend all of your time working two jobs in a bid to increase your income, it's going to leave very little time for you to spend with your family. This isn't an existence that any of us wants. Thus, you not only need to increase your income, but you need to increase it in a way whereby your time available remains roughly the same.

In short, you need to leverage your time.

TIME LEVERAGE

Bill Gates was one of the first people to openly talk about the importance of leveraging time. As he put it, he'd rather spend his days doing the things he enjoyed doing, whether it made him money or not. These days, that happens to be pondering over the problems the developing world faces such as education, clean drinking water, and so on. As you can imagine, there's no money in building pipes in an underdeveloped country.

Gates' point was his income is not connected to his time anymore. He has enough money to the point where it multiplies all by itself and even a small return is huge enough for him to get by pretty easily, even by his standards. The good news from all of this is that you don't need to be as rich as Gates to achieve this reality.

You too can create a situation where your money makes money and enables you to live easily. It all begins with divorcing your time and income earning ability. Most of us trade our time for money. You might think of it as you being paid for your expertise but the reality is that you're devoting a certain number of hours to your employer and in return, you receive a paycheck.

Even those working white collar jobs are in this situation. Ask yourself what would happen if you showed up for work just two hours per day and still managed to get all of your tasks done? Would your boss be okay with this? Something tells me the first thing they'll do is insist you show up on time and remain at work for eight hours and the next thing they'll do is load you with more work since you're just so efficient.

You can think of income that is connected to time as being active income. A business can also be active and time-centric. Think of a freelancer who writes words for a living. In this case, they're being compensated per word, but those words take time to produce. The quicker they can produce those words, the more they get paid at the end of the month.

Other time-centric businesses include operating a physical retail store of some kind. You will need to devote time to running it every single day and you cannot sit back and let it run itself. More likely than not, your store employees will become demotivated and start getting ideas in their head, none of which are good for your business.

Active income by itself isn't bad, but it does require a time commitment. Generally, it's great to have an active source of income since this keeps you busy. Even after you're financially independent, you don't need to give up your active income source since everyone needs something to do. An active income source provides structure and if you really enjoy the work you do, it provides meaning as well.

However, active sources are not what we're after when we're looking to increase our income.

Passive Income

Passive income is the opposite of active income. A

passive source is one where time spent and money earned as disconnected from one another. There are few truly passive income sources available for you to take advantage of. A truly passive source is one where you invest your money and it goes away and grows all by itself.

A bank savings account or a certificate of deposit (CD) is an example of a truly passive income source. You don't need to do anything. The downside is that the rates of return are pretty low (pathetic even) and you'll need a large principal invested in these in order to be able to live off the returns.

Most opportunities that are available fall somewhere in between the active and passive spectrum. With these avenues, the money making bit is not connected to time spent, however, you do need to spend time setting things up in the first place. Thus you can't think of them as being completely passive but the good news is that they behave much like snowballs do.

You'll need to devote time at first but once the snow-ball gets rolling, it takes very little corrective action to ensure it keeps its momentum and size. Some of the ideas presented in the next section are examples of such avenues. I'd like to mention at this point that these opportunities are businesses by themselves. If you have a mental block against opening a business or think that you don't have what it takes, remember what I mentioned earlier.

The nature of business these days is very different from what it used to be. You don't need to sit behind a counter and count every single penny or manage employees to run a successful business anymore. You can be a one (wo)man show and earn income passively.

Before we move onto the ways to make passive income, let's take a look at another important concept with regards to time leverage.

Compounding

Albert Einstein once said that compounding was the eight wonder of the world. It is astonishing to think how underestimated compounding truly is. All of us have a basic idea of how it works but the ramifications of it are hard to grasp because our brains don't function that way.

The basic premise of compounding is easy to visualize. 4% of 1,000 is far less than 4% of 10,000,000. In the latter case, you can live pretty easily off those returns, but the former amount will buy you a decent meal and that's about it. The thing about compounding is that as those 4% returns are reinvested into the principal, both your principal and returns grow exponentially (as opposed to a linear manner.)

This means the longer you leave your principal untouched, the more money you'll make. You've already seen an example of compounding back in the first chapter when you saw how drastically the savings of our 21 year old college grad changed when we withdrew money for certain needs, or how the principal values stood at various points in time.

Compounding is the best way to leverage your time since it happens automatically. Therefore, you need to think of increasing your income as a structure where cash from one source goes into a compounding structure that goes away and does its thing, without any need for you to interfere. An example of this would be a side hustle that produces excess cash that is diverted into a stock market investment that returns 7% on average over time.

My point is that you should focus on creating passive income structures which are grounded by the power of compounding. This is opposed to a view where you look at creating passive income sources. A source is a standalone thing that may or may not be powerful for your bottom line. A structure implies resilience and efficiency.

With all of this being said, let's take a look at some realistic ways you can increase your income.

. . .

Ways to Increase **Your Income**

The methods outlined here are both active and passive in nature. As such, I'm not going to bore you with savings accounts or CDs since you already know about those. Instead, I'm going to focus on creating higher levels of cash flow.

Driving For Ridesharing Companies

Despite the stick that these companies, such as Uber and Lyft, receive, the fact is that they remain a good source of secondary income. The downside is that you'll need to buy a car and you'll have to devote time to this. This means you'll have to incur a double whammy of taking on both debt and devoting time to it.

However, careful considerations of the economics of the job will result in free cash flowing into your pocket. The primary consideration for you is the loan terms for your vehicle. You can't get away with buying a cheap beater since you're unlikely to qualify as a service provider.

Furthermore, when was the last time you got into a cab that looked less than new? The best thing to do is to get yourself a vehicle with as low monthly payments as you can possibly get away with and still qualify to drive for these companies. Before getting a loan, you'll need to estimate how much you could make in terms of revenue and whether it's worth your while.

You can use the calculator at https://www.finder.com/ uber-income to plug in numbers and check whether things match up. Here are some of the assumptions I made. Keep in mind that I've considered worst case scenario numbers:

- Working hours per week -30
- Average rate per hour - $10 (will be far higher in metro areas)
- Gas expense - $150 per month
- Maintenance - $100 per month
- Miscellaneous items - $50 per month
- Car insurance - $250 per month
- Car payment (if applicable) - $350 per month

These numbers result in a monthly income of $254 after taxes. Remove the car payment portion and you'll end up $550 per month in additional income. This is $6600 per year which is a decent amount. Also keep in mind that this is after we've assumed numbers that are higher on average in terms of expenses.

The major issue here is the amount of time you wish to devote to driving your vehicle. The other issue is that while average hourly earnings for major cities are far higher than the $10 I've assumed in this calculation, the fact is that you're not going to find passengers at all times. This makes the income unsteady.

Selling Items Online - Retail Arbitrage

While you can sell the stuff you already own and don't need online for cash, this isn't a very reliable source of income. Instead, what you can do is practice what is called retail arbitrage. I'll be honest, in the previous decade this was one of the easiest ways to make money but these days, you'll need to devote some time to search for the ideal products.

Arbitrage refers to taking advantage of different prices that similar products have. The way retail arbitrage works is when you find a product that is listed for $10 on Amazon (for example) and resell it for $20 on Ebay thanks to the auction process inflating prices. It sounds simple but the fact is that the number of opportunities these days are low and in very niche products.

As a result, it takes time to break in and you'll have to spend significant amounts of time devoted to researching prices. In addition to this you'll need to spend time driving around sourcing items that you can arbitrage. These days, the most profitable method of retail arbitrage is to use Amazon FBA.

FBA stands for Fulfilled by Amazon and this is how the entire process works. It begins with you scouring

Goodwill and thrift stores for items that you can potentially sell on Amazon. Once you locate a particular item, you can check what the lowest price it is being offered for an Amazon. If you have at least a 20% gross profit on the price you'll pay to buy the item and the lowest price on Amazon, you have a winner.

I must mention that this is not an easy business to undertake. It requires a lot of time and effort to put into action and it isn't something that will yield a huge return immediately. There is a time investment here and given that it's a business, your returns are not guaranteed. However, if you can automate the process, it isn't unheard of for people to earn upwards of $3,000 per month practicing this.

One way of automating this is by sourcing product lists. There are a number of services that offer newsletter (for a price) full of products that list items that you can arbitrage on Amazon. The FBA part comes in when you order the product and ship it directly to Amazon's warehouses. They'll take care of the shipping and handling as well as any returns that might occur.

There are some downsides to this business that you should be aware of: First, Amazon is going to eventually compete with you on your bestselling items. As a big corporation, Amazon exists to make money and one way they do this is by accessing seller data on their platform. If you happen to have a product that is a consistent bestseller, don't be surprised to see Amazon lowball your product with their own branded product, even if it comes from the same factory.

Next, there are many ways you can screw this up and it takes time to get good at it. This might mean it's just too much work for you to undertake. There's another way of looking at this though. If you keep at it, your competition will eventually whittle itself away and you'll manage to succeed.

Success in this field is a matter of persistence and consistency. You can refer to websites like https://onlinesellingexperiment.com/retail-arbitrage-2/ to learn more about this business.

YOUTUBE AND SOCIAL *Media Channels*

While the prior methods had you moving up and around trying to generate cash, this method is something you can do right from your home. In addition to this, this is also a largely passive method of earning money which means your income is dissociated from the time spent on your tasks.

Youtube has been around for many years now and it has become one of the best ways to generate eyeballs. The way to do this is to produce content that people love to watch. Once you begin to receive traffic, you can monetize the channel by using affiliate marketing (which you'll learn next) or by selling your own courses and products.

The key is to find a topic that people want to consume content on and matching that with your ability to create said content. You'll have to find very specific niches to make this work since the broad niches such as travel, money, sports, and politics are saturated. I mean, it's unlikely that you're going to be able to compete against the likes of CNN, Forbes, and huge travel companies when it comes to content. To be frank, finding your niche is the most daunting portion of the entire process. It is tough to figure out what you want to talk about and whether people will want to listen to it.

It's not just Youtube you can create content on. Other social media channels such as Instagram, Pinterest, and Snapchat are great ways to drive traffic to your preferred sales outlet. It takes time to build great content and grow a following but with persistence, you'll get there.

The good news is that once your traffic snowball starts building, it'll become hard to stop and will require little maintenance on your part. All you'll need to do is respond with good content at the frequency your audience demands and the rest will take care of itself.

The other great thing about making money this way is the sheer number of avenues you have to sell. You can create an online store where you can sell merchandise using print on demand services such as Teespring, you can create online courses on the topic and sell them on Udemy, you can write a book and sell it via Amazon's Kindle publishing platform or you can setup a simple website of your own and sell it directly on there.

The possibilities are endless. The trick is to take the time to identify your niche and not hurry things. Make a list of all the things you're good at or know about. In addition to this, include topics you're willing to do the research on and have been curious about for a while. Remember, people online are not necessarily looking for an expert.

Great content can also be someone talking at the level of the audience member. If you've always been curious about the physics of space but aren't a physics major, creating a channel where you discuss these phenomena will be a huge attraction and your viewers will feel as if they can relate to you really well.

Don't get too caught up in the specifics of monetization. Once you build your traffic, you'll find that monetization methods will make themselves known to you. Focus on your content and the rest will take care of itself.

Affiliate Marketing

Affiliate marketing is a fancy term that means you'll be selling things online for a commission. You can sell physical products or you can sell software and courses. There is no limit to how and what you wish to sell. As with the previous method, the key is to be able to generate high levels of traffic. Every time someone buys the product you recommend, you receive a commission.

The best way to find products to sell is to signup for affiliate marketplaces (also called affiliate networks). These are places where merchants list their products along with the commissions they will pay for a sale. The most popular affiliate marketplace is Amazon Associates. By signing up to this, you can promote any product that is sold on Amazon.

Other popular networks include Clickbank, CJ Affiliate, and Shareasale. In addition to this, many business owners have their own affiliate programs. Every merchant has different requirements but it's pretty easy to get approved for a lot of programs even if you don't have a website.

The real trick lies in figuring out how you'll drive traffic to your sales pages. As I mentioned, you can sell products through your Youtube channel or your website. As always, great content is key. This is what pulls people in and gets them to trust you enough to go ahead and click the link you place to the product.

Other Ways of Making Money

There are other ways of making money in your spare time but understand that these will never fully replace your primary income the way a business potentially can. The flip side is that these are easy to get started with and you'll earn money pretty much right away. Taking surveys and completing odd jobs via platforms such as Taskrabbit or Amazon's Mechanical Turk can bring in an additional $70-100 per month.

You can also make money taking surveys via platforms such as Swagbucks which happens to be the most popular platform for such things. Another great way to make money is to test websites. Using platforms such as Usefeel.com or Usertesting.com, you can earn money to simply navigate through websites and talk your thoughts out loud.

The number of ways to make money online is unlimited. In addition to the methods outlined here, there are other ways you can increase your income. Don't rush into any of them and take your time to think about it and choose the best one for you.

8

INVESTMENT STRATEGIES FOR ANY
FINANCIAL SITUATION

*W*here are you going to invest all of that extra income you make and how will you get your compound interest machine rolling? This is the subject of this chapter. Successful investing lies at the heart of financial independence and you need to learn how to do this. The good news is that investing successfully is a lot simpler than you think.

I say simple and not easy because most people trip themselves up by trying to get too smart with their strategies. Before we get into the specifics of this chapter, I'd like to point out that I'm not a certified financial advisor; these are just my opinions. You should always consult a professional and do your own research prior to investing money in the markets.

Another thing I'd like to point out is that you should be

carrying out these strategies only once you've managed to eliminate all of your debt.

STOCK MARKET INVESTING SIMPLIFIED

There is no shortage of material devoted to stock market investing. It is a topic that has consumed many ever since companies could list their shares for the public to buy. There have been many different strategies proposed but there's no denying the fact that over the long term, the best one has been to simply buy and hold for as long as possible.

In fact, this is the same strategy that Warren Buffett, whom many consider to be the greatest investor of all time, follows. There are many other nuances to what Buffett does obviously, but the fact remains that buying stocks and holding them for as long as possible is the bedrock of what he does.

The big question at this point is: Should you buy individual stocks or should you focus on buying index funds that track market index performance? Buying individual stocks is the same as buying a share in a business. Imagine if your local grocery store owner approached you one day and asked you to invest money in his store in exchange for a share of the profits. Would you agree to this?

Your answer depends on some combination of your knowledge of that particular business and your risk tolerance when it comes to investing. Generally speaking, investing in individual shares is a risky proposition. This is because companies face a multitude of risks and there are many moving parts to a successful business.

Over and above this, you can buy an already successful business but how do you know what it's going to be worth in a few years' time? You might be buying the stock at a high price that might not be matched ever again thanks to the business being wildly overvalued. Such risks are massively magnified when purchasing individual stocks.

SIMPLIFY

The common approach to deciphering the stock market is to complicate matters and to treat the market as if it's an extremely complicated black box. This might be true, as complicated strategies require you to spend a large amount of time on them. In the big picture of leveraging time, this income model doesn't make sense for you to get into.

After all, it takes a long time to properly analyze a business' prospects and people usually spend studying equity valuation in business schools. The thing for you to do instead is to simplify your approach and make it easy for yourself.

This is why index fund investing is the best choice for most people. You can simply track the broader market's performance and capture all gains in your portfolio. Best of all, you need to buy just one security and not an entire basket's worth of stocks. Over the long term, your portfolio will match the performance of the stock market.

As mentioned earlier, the American stock market has averaged 7% per year since the late 1800's. There is also greater security in investing in the entire stock market. The reason is that if the stock market comes crashing down over a long period of time, you're likely to have far bigger problems on hand than just worrying about your portfolio.

What I mean is that if the American stock markets are no longer viable investment destinations, this probably means that America's prospects as a strong nation itself are in jeopardy. Given the position America is in right now, this seems to be a remote possibility. Even if it does occur, there will probably be far bigger issues to worry about than just the stock market.

Costs

When it comes to investing in funds you have two choices: index funds or mutual funds. Mutual funds are managed actively. This is to say that there is a dedicated manager who decides on the individual stock weight in the portfolio and maintains the portfolio accordingly.

Mutual funds also have far more specific objectives than index funds. For example, you can buy mutual funds that aim to capture the gains from high yielding bonds. There are other mutual funds that seek to capture the rise in foreign tech company stocks and so on. There really is no limit to the mandate that mutual funds can have.

The flip side is that mutual funds have a raft of fees associated with them. Generally, these amount to at least two percent of your gains. This means that the mutual fund you invest in has to outperform the general market by at least two percent in order for you to make money. This might not sound like much but is actually a significant hurdle for money managers to overcome over a long period of time.

Index funds don't have this issue since they're largely managed by algorithms that buy and sell stocks to maintain the same composition of the index they track. Thus the fees of the average index fund is exceedingly low, often less than 0.5% of your gains. This means your hurdle rate is far lower and is much more manageable.

You might argue that an index fund always matches the

index performance and thus the investor always realizes a slight underperformance after fees. This is true. However, consider that an index fund is guaranteed to match that performance. A mutual fund on the other hand can outperform but also drastically underperform the index.

Historically, most mutual funds tend to underperform broader market indices. sure there are funds that have managed to outperform the market even after fees but these are few and far in between. Generally speaking, your money is a lot safer in an index fund since you're guaranteed to at least match the average market performance.

How to Invest

The best way to get started is to open a zero commission brokerage account like those offered by M1 Finance and a number of other brokers such as Charles Schwab. The next step is to purchase a low cost index fund from the likes of Vanguard or Fidelity. These organizations have been around for a long time and offer a wide variety of funds that offer a low cost way of capturing market performance.

Don't run wild here and buy a fund that tracks the performance of developing markets or something exotic. Stick to the basics and simply purchase an index fund that tracks the performance of the American stock market.

A common question at this point is to wonder whether it's better to invest a lump sum into the market or is it better to invest amounts every single month. The latter method is called Dollar Cost Averaging or DCA. The objective of DCA is to develop greater discipline around investing and to ensure that your money goes automatically into the market, on schedule.

The issue really comes down to commissions. If you're operating a zero fee account then either method will work for you. However, if commissions are involved, a lump sum investing strategy will work best. This is because a lot of brokers charge flat fees and these can add up with regular purchases. The key to making money in stocks is to reduce fees to almost zero.

Once you've invested your money, you simply need to sit back and continue investing at regular intervals. If you're investing via a lump sum method, fix a sum and once it accumulates, invest it into the index fund. As such, you don't need to monitor the price or your unrealized gains since what can you possibly do about this?

Keep investing simple and you'll find that your money will grow in lockstep with the market. A great way to do this is to implement this program in your 401(k) or retirement accounts. If your employer matches your contributions then this is even better.

REAL ESTATE STRATEGY

There are two ways for you to invest in real estate. The first is to invest in financial securities called REITs which I mentioned earlier. A REIT is a company that owns large tracts of real estate such as malls, commercial buildings, apartment buildings etc. By purchasing shares of a REIT, you are purchasing a share of the rental income from the underlying properties.

REITs are required by law to distribute 90% of their income to their investors and as a result, you will earn a pretty sizable cash yield on your investment. REITs typically yield around 7-8% before taxes on their share prices. If you don't have enough money saved up to purchase a piece of real estate, then REITs are a great, low cost way to enter the real estate market.

Once you do have enough money saved up though, it makes sense to acquire a piece of real estate for yourself. The key is to maximize capital gains as well as cash flow from it in order for it to be a true asset. After all, you'll be drawing a mortgage on the property and you want it to be leveraged and not debt.

The first question is: How much do you need to buy real estate? The short answer is that you'll need to pay the down payment, fees, and closing costs on a mortgage. This amount usually equals around 30% of the total value of the property with 20% being the down payment you need to make.

You can pay less as a down payment but you'll often have to bear additional costs if you do this. Also, some lenders might stick you with higher interest rates than normal. The exception to this are FHA loans that require down payments as little as 3.5% if your credit score is good enough (580 or higher.) The average FHA loan can be had for as little as 10% down.

You've already read about house hacking previously and how this builds your net worth. One of the best ways to turbocharge the house hacking strategy is to incorporate it into what is referred to as a Buy, Rehab, Rent, Refinance, and Repeat strategy.

More House Hacking Strategies

Buy, Rehab, Rent, Refinance, and Repeat. This is a great strategy that works wonders for your net worth. The downside is that it can be a little complicated for a beginner so let's look at this in more detail. The first step of the process is called buy and this is easy enough to understand.

The key is to scout for properties that need some fixing up. You're not going to be in the market for that shiny, new single family home. Single family homes are your typical suburban homes that are occupied by, you guessed, single families. Instead, you'll be on the lookout for what are called multi family units that need some sprucing up.

This is what the second step refers to. Rehab is where you put some money into the property to make it livable so that its market value will increase once repairs are carried out. You want to be careful here and choose a property that you can realistically repair. Too often, first time buyers go out and buy a property that has far too many holes in it to fix.

The reason you want to search for properties that need fixing up is that you're guaranteed a profit as soon as the sale closes. If you find a property that can be worth $155,000 once fixed up (repairs costing you $10,000) but are able to purchase it for $100,000, that's a $45,000 profit the minute you're done rehabbing the place.

This method has a lot of advantages for first time home buyers as well. This is because the FHA (Federal Housing Authority) has special loans designated 203(k) which is aimed at loaning money to first time home buyers who require money to fix up a piece of property. The benefits are the same as the ones outlined previously where your down payment amounts can be as low as three percent.

The next step is to rent the place out. Remember you're buying multi family units such as an apartment complex. Don't get intimidated by the word complex, a building with four units is also referred to as such. You'll occupy one unit while renting out the other three. There are a lot of nuances to renting and finding good tenants so make sure to do your research and educate yourself on how you can best position your property.

The last step is to carry out what's called a cash out refinance. This is a complex process but briefly here's how it works. Once you've built up a certain amount of equity (your lender or institution will define this for you), you can refinance your mortgage. Since your home value has increased, the loan amount will be greater, but thanks to the amount you owe remaining the same, the balance is paid out to you in cash.

This way, you're now free to go ahead and repeat the process with another piece of property. For more information on how BRRRR works and various tips and tricks visit https://investfourmore.com/brrrr-method/ . In addition to this, you can learn more about the FHA and its loan offerings at https://www.homebridge.com/renovation-lending/fha-203k-loan/eligibility-requirements/

Make sure to carry out your research thoroughly before committing to this strategy. It can seem intimidating but the presence of trained professionals every step of the way will ensure that you'll never be caught doing the wrong thing. Of course, this doesn't mean you're guaranteed a profit but at the very least you'll learn how things ought to be done.

9

TRAVEL FOR FREE

I promised you I'd show you how to travel for free and we're finally here. There are a number of travel hacks you can employ to ensure you pay far less than the sticker price for flights, hotels, and other holiday-related expenses. This chapter will give you the lowdown on how I travel for next to nothing and how you can do so as well!

TRAVEL HACKING

Travel hacking is something that a lot of people want to do but very few manage to do it well. The fact is that it really isn't that difficult these days to earn rewards you can apply toward flights or hotel stays. However, doing it well is another thing entirely. Often people misuse their rewards points and spend them on things that don't offer the best possible reward.

Before getting into travel hacking, I must mention that if you have a debt to clear, this should be your number one priority. In order to earn points and free flights etc., you need to have excellent credit and this is not possible if you have a debt to clear. So focus on the important things first before trying to score free flights and the like.

Another thing I'd like to point out is that a lot of people seem to think of points and miles as earning something for nothing. In other words, there is a tendency in people to think that earning miles and rewards points is as simple as opening an account with a bank or a credit card and free trips follow.

This is not really the case. You will need to spend money in order to earn these rewards. You will receive signup bonuses but these don't count for much in the overall picture. So don't expect a miracle here. Think of these rewards as being an added bonus when you spend money. For example, if you use your debit card to buy groceries, all you're receiving in return are groceries.

With the right credit card, you'll receive your groceries as well as a fraction of a free trip to Hawaii, for instance. It's about the return you receive on your regular spending, not a free lunch.

. . .

THE BASICS

The world of rewards and points has its own lingo so it's worth spending some time dissecting this. It can seem complicated from the outside but this really isn't the case. To begin with, rewards can be called either miles or points. Miles are offered on credit cards that are connected to an airline such as United or Delta.

In the US, there are three big carriers (United Airlines, Delta, and American Airlines) along with Southwest which is the biggest budget airline. These airlines partner with banks to issue credit cards that reward you with miles for every dollar you spend. The ratio of miles received to dollars spent varies. For example, you could receive one mile for every dollar spent or a ¼ mile for every dollar.

This ratio varies depending on the airline and the card, so you'll need to check individual offers to determine this. The other type of rewards you can earn are points. Points are usually issued on travel-themed credit cards and can be reimbursed to pay for hotel stays or flights. Generally speaking, cards that issue points are more versatile but this is not always the case as I'll shortly explain.

The points you receive will be fixed at a certain ratio to the dollars you spend as well as to the miles you'll receive on an airline and the nights you'll receive at a partner hotel. For example, 100 points might net you 10 miles on Delta and one night at Marriott or two nights at a lower priced chain of the Marriott group.

This can get confusing but most credit card websites have calculators that display the value of your redeemed points. There is a third type of credit card reward that some people prefer. This is the cashback credit card. Cashback is the most versatile since you can choose how you'd like to redeem your rewards. These are not necessarily travel-themed, but you can use them towards travel.

Some cashback credit cards offer perks such as the use of lounges at airports around the world. Airlines and hotels aren't standalone entities and operate on the basis of alliances. When it comes to airlines there are three major alliances: Star alliance, Oneworld alliance, and Skyteam. Every airline in the world will be a part of one of these alliances.

Thus, if you have rewards that can earn you miles on Delta, you can use those miles to book flights on Alitalia for a vacation in Italy (Alitalia and Delta are a part of Skyteam.) In essence, the whole world opens itself up to you thanks to such alliances. Hotels don't partner up with one another to such a large extent but given that they operate on a franchisee basis, major chains such as Hilton, Marriott, Sheraton etc have resorts all around the world.

Hotels tend to have different chains under their umbrella depending on the type of luxury they offer. For example, the Marriott chain has Courtyard, Marriott, and JW Marriot among others under its umbrella. Courtyard is the lowest priced while JW is usually the highest priced. You will find that in some countries, the service level differs. For example, in the US, Courtyard Marriotts are thought of as being high class motels but in India, they're bonafide five star hotels.

In other places, the chains will bestow different names to their brands. Sticking with Marriott, in some places they designate their highest end hotels as being JW Marriott Marquis as opposed to simply JW Marriott. The points you earn will net you a different number of nights depending on the brand you choose within their umbrella.

Still with me? Great! Let's look at a few things which are slightly more advanced.

TRANSFERS AND REDEMPTION

The way to earn points is to apply for and receive a credit card with a bank. The most popular bank for travel-themed credit cards is Chase. Given the volume of applications they received when they first introduced their cards, Chase instituted a policy which is unofficially referred to as the 5/24 rule.

5/24 means that any person who is applying for a card cannot have opened more than five credit cards within the previous two years (24 months.) When the time comes to apply for credit cards, it's best to apply for Chase first before you move on to American Express or Citi.

A word of caution: As I've mentioned earlier, in the wrong hands, credit cards can be veritable WMDs for your money. The marketing for credit cards is extremely strong and you'll be tempted to open a card account with every bank under the sun thanks to the rewards they offer.

It is just bad practice to open a large number of credit card accounts. Opening an account solely for the rewards on offer is a good idea only when you have a good handle on your spending. If you want to earn rewards, it's best to open one or two card accounts and concentrate your spending on those cards instead of spreading them out. This way, you'll actually spend enough to earn rewards, instead of accumulating small rewards everywhere that don't add up to much.

A lot of cards offer the ability to transfer points. For example, if you have a Delta branded card that has earned you 1,000 miles, you can sometimes transfer this to earn points that count towards a hotel stay. The ratio at which these miles convert into nights will vary depending on the credit card you apply for.

You can spend an eternity dissecting the best cards and rewards programs but unless you have some special loyalty towards a brand or a company, it's best to stick to either Chase or American Express credit cards. Amex tends to offer luxury-themed rewards and their points stack up to a lot less than with Chase. However, this is because Amex points get you a lot more so it evens out.

The only downside with Amex is that they aren't accepted everywhere and if you travel abroad a lot, it's going to be tough to find a merchant that accepts them. In contrast, Chase's cards are all based off the Visa platform and as such, merchants have no problems accepting them.

REDEMPTION RULES

There aren't too many rules for you to follow in order to redeem your points smartly. The biggest rule you need to keep in mind is that you should not redeem your points when a straight cash purchase will cost you less. For example, if you receive 10 miles for every $100 spent on a Delta branded credit card, this makes every mile worth $10.

Consider that you have 500 miles or $5,000 on your card and you want to fly to New York City (let's say you live in Columbus, OH). If a flight ticket costs you $300 both ways, it makes no sense to redeem your miles toward a flight. This is a hypothetical scenario which is why there's such a huge difference in numbers. In reality, you'll see them being a lot closer.

The other rule that you need to follow is that you should never get into debt trying to earn rewards. In other words, pay off your balance in full every month and do not put yourself in a position where you'll need to carry balances over. Do not spend more than what you can afford. This is why it's critical for you to eliminate all of your debt before you even think about applying for credit cards.

Maintaining your credit score is essential in order to be able to really take advantage of the rewards on offer. Often, applying for rewards-based credit cards will enhance your overall score. This happens due to the vagaries of the way your credit report is built. Everybody's credit report has a metric that measures your total credit usage. For example, if you have two credit cards and have unpaid balances on both, your credit usage is higher than someone who has three cards and has no balance on either of them.

By applying for two cards (as recommended previously) and paying off the balance in full, your total credit usage will always be low. This means your credit score receives a boost. If you have old credit card accounts that have a zero balance and are inactive, don't close these accounts. You may not be using them but their zero balances contribute to boosting your overall score.

As long as you monitor those accounts for fraudulent usage, you'll be just fine. The best way to make sure your credit report is up to scratch is to simply practice prudent financial behavior. Don't spend more than what you can afford and pay off your balances in full at all times.

As you can see, using credit cards prudently can add a lot more than just money back in your pocket. However, it takes time to build up to this so don't go out and apply for credit cards until you've built up a buffer of emergency money. This is an amount equivalent to six months' worth of expenses as well as a sum that you figure will pay for any emergencies.

In terms of priorities, credit cards are low and you can be fully financially independent without them. They're a bit like the cherry on top of the cake so you don't need them per se.

10

THE DRAWDOWN - CROSSING THE FINISH LINE

*Y*ou've finally made it all the way here! After all that talk of income versus debt and building assets and reducing liabilities, it's now time to talk about how you're going to spend your money in retirement. The exact way you'll be spending this depends on when you plan on retiring of course.

If you're one of the lucky (and well prepared) ones who will be retiring well before the usual 'retirement' age, you will need to devote time to planning out exactly how you can redeem your funds to pay for your expenses. Let's look at the various elements that go into this decision.

RETIREMENT ACCOUNTS

The first piece of the puzzle is figuring out which accounts you'll draw from first. There is a tax bill that comes with drawing down your tax deferred accounts and it is in your best fiscal interest to delay this as much as possible. This depends on your individual situation, so take some time to work the numbers.

A good option to implement is to divert income such as dividends from your investments into your checking account instead of reinvesting them back into stock purchases. Again, you should do this only if you need the cash flow. A lot of people choose to keep working in some form or fashion so you need not necessarily do this.

Remember that our calculations that have preceded this chapter have assumed a long term portfolio return of seven percent before taxes so the longer you leave this money untouched the better. A good option at this point is to withdraw a greater percentage of your passive income streams and turn that into cash flow to pay for your expenses.

.   .   .

Goals

Remember that the key piece of the puzzle is to figure out what kind of lifestyle you want in retirement. I'm using retirement as a state of mind here and not necessarily as a lifestyle where you don't work anymore. As I mentioned earlier, you can pretty much retire when you have enough money in the bank to not necessarily work anymore or require a particular job as an income stream.

Your retirement income calculations hinge on the costs that this lifestyle requires so it is important that you take the time to figure this out well in advance. Remember to add a suitable buffer for whatever monthly expenses you project. Also, remember that you don't need to necessarily retire in the US.

There are a growing number of places abroad that have the facilities of a developed country but a fraction of the cost of living. More often than not, as long as you can prove that you have a steady income stream, it is possible to live long term on a retirement visa. So research your options thoroughly and remember that the entire world is open to you!

Remember that you'll be withdrawing four percent of your nest egg as detailed in the previous chapters. Ideally, you'll have a 50% stock and bond mix in your portfolio but this isn't a hard and fast rule. It's true that as you get older, a larger bond presence in your portfolio will stabilize it better but it comes down to what your risk tolerance is.

Bonds will give you steady but lower returns while stocks are more likely to hit the 7% projected return figure more easily. However, they can be volatile in the short term. A good way to insulate yourself from the short term fluctuations of the market is to establish a passive income business as detailed previously. This will ensure that you'll ride out the short term panic better.

HEALTHCARE

The biggest expense you'll be dealing with during retirement is the cost of healthcare for you and your partner as applicable. The cost of private health insurance will be a lot higher than whatever your employer will provide you with so make sure to research what this amount will cost.

Truth be told, there's no way to get a fully accurate figure of what this amount will be, so a ballpark figure will have to do. In addition to this, you should also consider drawing life insurance policies in your name to avoid saddling your dependants with costs upon death or any adverse conditions that might occur.

. . .

Mindset

If you choose to live entirely off your nest egg and not work at all, there will be feelings of vulnerability when you see your portfolio move up and down according to the market's whims. The worst case scenario is if you happen to run into a stock market crisis where you lose a large portion of your principal and all of a sudden, you're faced with a massive reduction in income.

These are the risks you'll have to undertake and there's no way to get rid of them completely. The best you can do is build an appropriate margin of safety into your expenses. The next best thing to do is to establish an income source that is not dependent on your nest egg. A side hustle or some part time work that you can do are excellent options to pursue.

This is why I mentioned earlier that it is important and more beneficial in the long term for you to set up a side business that earns money by itself with minimal maintenance on your part. Sure, you might lose some money trying to figure out how to do things correctly, but the amount you'll lose compared to the massive amounts of security you will receive in the long run makes it a worthwhile risk to take.

Most people figure this out far too late in their lives. This is also why leverage is such a smart play when it comes to real estate. If you seek to eschew borrowing money completely and don't differentiate between debt and leverage, you're unlikely to over invest in rental properties in your lifetime. This cuts off a major source of cash flow for you in retirement.

As you can see, the drawdown period doesn't have any major nuances to it. It all depends on how well you set up the preceding steps. Do the right things and build appropriate margins of safety and you'll find that everything will go smoothly, even if the rest of the financial world is falling apart in the short term.

Retirement is a scary word for a lot of people. This happens because of a lack of preparation and because most people get intimidated by the very thought of it. Financial independence is the real goal here instead of merely seeking a 'comfortable' retirement. The fact is that thanks to the unfortunate events of the previous decade, more Americans than ever are grossly unprepared for retirement.

There are two ways of viewing these events. The first, and mainstream way of examining them is to view them as a disaster that wiped out portfolios and consigned an entire generation of Americans to work forever. There is a lot of truth in this viewpoint. The millennial generation has seen an extraordinary amount of change and disruption in their lifetimes.

A person born in the late 80s to early 90s has witnessed

two full stock market collapses, the worst ever terrorist attack on American soil, technological advances that have rendered a number of jobs obsolete, and a changing work environment where people are viewed as resources more than ever, coupled with the erosion of benefits that previous generations took for granted.

When seen this way, it shouldn't come as a surprise that people these days don't trust corporations or the stock markets. However, there is an alternate view. Instead of viewing this chaos as being solely bad, one can view it as presenting a number of opportunities. The two stock market crashes that occurred created losses but they also gave rise to two of the longest bullish stretches in American financial history, the second of which is still running as of this writing.

While it is entirely possible to lose money in those crashes, it was equally possible to make money in them. Which side of the market you landed on depended on the principles you followed at the time. This much is true: The world is far more unstable now and you can expect more crises to occur.

However, every crisis brings with it the seed of opportunity. Recognize the truth in this statement and you'll be better prepared to deal with the situation when it occurs. The best play to take advantage of such a situation is to sit and wait for them, while being conservative when there are no obvious opportunities available.

This means removing all need for excitement from your portfolio. If you feel the need to gamble, then allocate a small amount of money to do so and get it out of your system. Never make it your primary wealth building strategy. When making choices, remember that there is an opportunity cost inherent in everything thanks to time being finite. Always make choices that leverage your time the best and take part in plays where the odds lie in your favor.

Circle of Competence

A great way to make sure the odds of a situation favor you is to evaluate whether you have any expertise or edge in them. For example, if you know nothing about the stock market and don't know the difference between a balance sheet and a cash flow statement, it makes zero sense for you to be investing in individual stocks. You're far better chasing market average returns.

If you do have knowledge of these things and can evaluate a business well, then it would be remiss of you to not take advantage of your knowledge. Sure, there is greater risk involved but risk is also a function of how much you know about a situation. It is risky for a swimmer to take part in the 100m race in the Olympics. It is not risky for a 100m sprinter to do so.

You will hear a lot of blanket statements about the

stock market but remember to evaluate these from the standpoint of competence. Invest in yourself constantly via courses and other forms of knowledge, and you'll see your circle of competence grow exponentially.

I'm using the stock market as an example here. If you find that you're far more competent in the real estate market, you should invest in greater proportion into it. It's a bit like having a hot hand and betting low. When the odds are in your favor, you should bet heavily to extract maximum reward. Of course, you need to know how to evaluate the odds to begin with.

Be honest with yourself about the extent of your abilities and remember that most situations you'll encounter will probably not amount to much. What I mean is that you'll be presented with a variety of moments that will promise you a large return on your money or some obscene benefit. More often than not, these will not amount to much.

The truly great situations are the ones where you can reasonably predict outcomes and will be tied to the existing knowledge you have. Anything else is pure exaggeration. It is a pessimistic mindset to have, but it will protect you from losing your money in a lot of situations.

This isn't to say you should pigeon hole yourself into a particular niche and never venture out of it. Remember, this is where investing in yourself comes into play. I mean, you knew nothing about real estate when you were a kid. No one did when they were of that age. The foremost expert in the market spent time educating themselves in it and took the time to learn and gain experience.

Hence, focus on building your circle of competence and be conservatively average with your other options. While cutting expenses is important and powerful when pursuing financial independence, increasing your income is always more desirable.

Cutting Expenses

It is possible to focus far too much on this aspect of wealth building. It pays to pursue it aggressively but never at the cost of being unkind to yourself. Build large safety margins into your budget and you'll withstand most headwinds in life. You don't need to go ahead and indulge in every single one of your wants, but do indulge in some of them. It'll help keep you sane and bring a smile to your face. Nothing beats the simple pleasures of treating yourself every once in a while.

If you find a particular want itching away at you, prepare an outlet for its release. Thinking that indulging in that want is undisciplined is the wrong way to go about it. Instead, indulge in it in a disciplined manner without going overboard. For example, if you want a nice dress with matching shoes, buy a single dress and a pair of shoes. Don't go ahead and buy the entire store.

The point is to be happy. Money may not buy happiness but it sure does make it a lot easier to be happy. Remember that you are the master of your money—it works for you, not the other way around. Manage it well and you'll find that your life will become a lot easier.

When you do achieve financial independence, you'll thank yourself for all the discipline and methods you followed as outlined in this book. Fiscal independence might be a lot closer than you think, so start right away! No matter what your debt levels are or how far away you think freedom is, do something every day and every moment.

I guarantee you'll get there by following the methods you've learned in this book. I wish you all the luck and freedom in the world! Let me know how your journey goes and also when you achieve independence! I look forward to hearing your success story.